M000311466

PRINCIPLES OF
FINANCE

DANTES/DSST* Study Guide

© **2019 Breely Crush Publishing, LLC**

DSST is a registered trademark of The Thomson Corporation and its affiliated companies, and does not endorse this book.

971091918143

Published by Breely Crush Publishing, LLC
10808 River Front Parkway
South Jordan, UT 84095
www.breelycrushpublishing.com

ISBN-10: 1-61433-607-5
ISBN-13: 978-1-61433-607-5

Printed and bound in the United States of America.

DSST is a registered trademark of The Thomson Corporation and its affiliated companies, and does not endorse this book.

Table of Contents

Section 1.1: Fundamentals of Financial Statements

Financial statements are documents created through the accounting process, which are representations of the performance of a company over time. Users of financial statements are those within the company who use them to guide financial decision-making, as well as those outside of the company, such as investors, who use them to determine the financial health of the company and whether it is a good investment. Financial statements communicate a great deal of information about a company in a concise format. Key metrics from financial statements are also used in financial ratio analysis, which allows a company's financial performance to be standardized in order to compare performance of the same company over time, two companies in the same industry, or an individual company to the industry as a whole.

There are four main types of financial statements that we will review: the balance sheet, the income statement, the statement of cash flows, and the statement of owner's equity. It is critical that students understand how to recognize, read, as well as recreate these financial statements and understand each item they contain. We will look at each one in turn in order to familiarize ourselves with their structure and content.

SECTION 1.2: BALANCE SHEET

The balance sheet (which is also sometimes known as the statement of financial position) represents a snapshot of financial accounts at a single point in time. For example, you might receive a monthly statement for your bank accounts, which shows the balance ending on a specific date. Similarly, you might log on to your online accounts and check your balances on any particular day. Keep in mind that a balance is a result of actions you have taken over time to arrive at that particular balance. Your bank account balance at any point in time is a result of how much you have put into the bank account (usually earnings from wages or other income) and how much you have taken out. A balance sheet for a company is the same concept, only it contains many more account balances.

The main categories contained within the balance sheet are: assets, liabilities, and owner's equity. The assets of a company can be considered anything of tangible value (and sometimes intangible value, meaning it is not a physical item) owned by a company. In terms of the structure of the balance sheet, assets are usually listed on the left side of the balance sheet, and liabilities and owner's equity on the right side. You may occasionally see balance sheets where assets appear first, then liabilities, then owner's equity.

For example, think of the assets in your own life. Do you own a car? Do you own a home or collect items of value? These things are considered assets because they likely could be sold for some amount of money today if needed, or they might be utilized in the course of your work so you can generate income to live and "operate." The assets of a company are similar, in that they are valuable to the company because of their ability to generate sales in the operations of their business. Assets on the balance sheet are further subdivided into current assets and fixed assets. Current assets are cash or those assets we could reliably sell or convert to cash within a short period of time (usually less than one year's time). Another name for current assets is liquid assets. Current assets are items such as cash, marketable securities (securities that could be sold for cash quickly), inventory, prepaid expenses (such as prepayment of insurance for six months), and accounts receivable (these are generated when a company sells its products or services on credit).

There is also what is known as fixed assets, which are usually considered items such as buildings (as well as the furniture and fixtures inside them), land, machinery, and equipment (computers, software, etc.) needed to run the business. These are called fixed assets because they are meant to be utilized over a long period of time and they can also be much more difficult to convert to cash if needed. Think of a manufacturer of golf clubs, for example. The facilities and much of the machinery they use are very specific to their product and there may not likely be a market for golf club manufacturing equipment, should the company need to sell some assets to generate cash.

As we continue to learn about the categories contained on the balance sheet, it is important to understand the relationship between them. As mentioned above, assets are listed on the left, with liabilities and owner's equity on the right. This is because the assets of a business are financed by a mix of debt and equity, and this structure highlights the relationship: the total assets must equal total liabilities and owner's equity.

This is also known as the balance sheet equation:

Total assets = Total liabilities + Owner's Equity

We will look at some additional examples and equations at the end of this section. Because of this relationship, both sides of the balance sheet must be balanced. Therefore, the balance sheet not only shows what a company owns (its assets), but also how those assets are being financed. With this relationship in mind, let's review liabilities and owner's equity.

Liabilities are the debts of a company, which are also listed on the balance sheet in order of liquidity, that is, how soon they must be paid off. Current liabilities are those that are generally paid off within one year's time and include all types of short-term payables, such as accounts payable, payroll and income taxes payable, wages payable, and more. Payables are when a company still owes a supplier, employee, the government, or other entity money for an item, service, benefit, or expense. Using the example of accounts payable, you can think of it just as when you pay for something using a credit card. You purchased the item in the store, but you still owe the credit card company who extended the credit for you to do so. Just as with assets, liabilities can also be long-term in nature. When a company issues bonds in order to raise money for operating the business (raising capital), the principal balance is a long-term liability that will eventually need to be repaid. We usually classify long-term debt as anything greater than one year's duration.

The owner's equity section of the balance sheet shows the portion of assets financed by equity, and will list items such as preferred stock, common stock, capital paid in excess of par, and retained earnings. Preferred and common stock are two different types of stock with different rights given to the holder of the stock. Preferred stock is often referred to as a "hybrid" security because it has some features of debt and some features of stock. It is similar to debt in that the dividend is fixed, and preferred stockholders are entitled to dividends before common stockholders are entitled to them. Additionally, if a company were to go bankrupt, preferred stockholders would be entitled to any remaining proceeds from the sale of assets before common stockholders. However, unlike common stockholders, preferred stockholders often do not get voting rights.

Retained earnings are also listed in the owner's equity section, and represent the cumulative earnings (gains or losses minus dividends) since the beginning of the firm's operations. Capital paid in excess of par is a rather long name for a concept that deserves some explanation. Par value is the value placed on a share of stock when it is first listed for sale. For example, let's say that par value is $5. If the stock is very attractive to investors when it goes on sale, they might actually be willing to pay more for the right to own it, because there are always a limited number of shares of stock circulating at any time. So if someone pays $8 for a $5 par value stock, the capital in excess of par is: $8 - $5 = $3. This amount is still contained in the owner's equity accounts, but in a separate line item, to distinguish from the par value of the common stock.

As mentioned above, both sides of the balance sheet must balance, and we can use the balance sheet equation to determine the values in a missing account if we are supplied information from other accounts.

To use an example, let's say Bob's Boats, Inc. has total assets of $150 million, and total liabilities of $75 million. What would be the value of owner's equity?

Remember, Total assets (TA) = Total liabilities (TL) + Owner's Equity (OE), therefore:

$150 million = $75 million + OE

$150 million - $75 million = OE

OE = $75 million

Sheila's Windshield Wipers, Inc. recently issued some new common stock in order to pay off some long-term debt and their owner's equity account value is now $34 million. Their total assets are $72 million, what is the current value of their total debt?

$72 million = TL + $34 million

$72 million - $34 million = TL

TL = $38 million

Dave's Delicious Deli Co. has been working on getting their suppliers to extend more credit to them, and as a result, has increased their current liabilities to $50 million. If their owner's equity is worth $100 million, what is the value of their long-term liabilities and total liabilities?

$300 million = TL + $100 million

$300 million - $100 million = TL

TL = $200 million

TL = CL + LL

$200 million = $50 million + LL

$200 million - $50 million = LL

LL = $150 million

SECTION 1.3: INCOME STATEMENT

Let's move on to the income statement, which is also sometimes referred to as the profit and loss statement, because one of its main functions is to determine how profitable (or not) a company is. The first thing to notice about the income statement is that it measures the financial performance of a company over a specified period of time. The time period could be several months (such as a quarter), six months, a year, or longer, but generally income statements are generated in relation to some standard accounting period.

The top line of the income statement contains the revenues or sales during the time period being measured, and the first expense item follows cost of goods sold, or COGS. COGS are the inputs, such as the raw materials and components used to make a product for sale. When you deduct COGS you get gross profit. From there you deduct operating expenses, which are those that are not the direct inputs into the company's products, yet are required to operate the business, such as overhead, utilities, marketing, etc. These are also called selling, general, and administrative expenses (SG&A), which are deducted along with any depreciation expense the company may be entitled to in that period. Please note that a depreciation expense is not a cash expense (keep this in mind later when we discuss cash flows) and is a way to reduce overall income for tax purposes. At this point we arrive at operating income, which is sometimes referred to as earnings before interest and taxes (EBIT).

Now that we have determined operating profit, further deductions for items not directly related to operations, such as interest expense and taxes, are deducted. First, deducting interest expense gives us earnings before taxes (EBT) and then deducting taxes yields earnings after taxes (EAT), or net income. Net income is the "bottom line." From this point, if there were any dividends due to preferred stockholders, we would deduct them to determine earnings available to common stockholders.

Now that we have a basic understanding of the structure of the income statement, it is worth pointing out that income statements can be used to compare a company's performance over time. For example, if you were to generate income statements over consecutive time periods, such as four quarters in a row, or three to five years in a row, the purpose would be to reveal trends contained within the statement that can be gleaned over time. Comparing income statements over time can help to gauge growth, stagnation, or loss, as well as which section of the income statement is being affected. For example, if year over year revenues were increasing, yet total profits remain unchanged, it would be an indication that expenses are also increasing along with revenues. Perhaps cost of goods sold had to increase, or perhaps additional staff had to be hired to support the increase in sales, which is eating away at profits. It would be important to notice these types of changes, which can only be seen when comparing the income statement over time.

SECTION 1.4: STATEMENT OF CASH FLOWS

One thing that should be made clear is that there is a difference in how the income statement and balance sheet transactions are recorded from an accounting point of view, and for most firms, especially publicly traded firms, accounting is done on an accrual basis. This means that income or expenses are recognized as transactions take place, not necessarily just when cash actually changes hands, which is how most people think of income or expenses. That is why this concept may seem confusing if you have never encountered it before. Let's look at an example to illustrate. According to accounting rules, income can be recognized when services have been rendered (meaning, you completed the job you were hired to do) or goods delivered by the company. So if a company delivers $1 million worth of products to a retail store on day one, but they will not collect payment until day thirty, they are allowed to record $1 million in revenues (even though no cash has changed hands!). On the balance sheet they would also indicate they have $1 million in accounts receivable (money they are waiting to collect, or receive). This illustrates how revenues may not always coincide with time of cash flows received as payment.

It is for this reason that it should be clear why we need a statement of cash flows to translate the accrued items into cash transactions to ensure there is enough cash to carry on operations, or determine if additional funding is needed at any point in time. Using the above example, if you have recorded $1 million in revenues but do not know if it was in cash or accounts receivable, and someone outside the accounting department saw "$1 million dollar sale" and decided to purchase some new machinery needed for $500,000 cash, they would not be able to do so, unless that purchase was also on credit, using the $1 million in receivables as evidence of creditworthiness. If this all seems like a dangerous game of playing with numbers, then you have accurately assessed how crucially important the statement of cash flows really is. Without it, you will not have an accurate view of the solvency of your business (we will look at measures of solvency later).

In order to develop a statement of cash flows, the activities of the company can be broken down into three parts: cash flows from operating activities, cash flows from investing activities, and cash flows from financing activities.

Cash flows from operating activities is calculated as follows:

- Start with net income
- Add back depreciation (remember, this was a non-cash expense, simply a line item that reduces our income on the income statement, so we need to add back for cash purposes)
- Subtract any *increases* in current assets (for example, you purchase more inventory, inventory account increases, cash decreases)
- Add any *decreases* in current assets (using the same example, if inventory decreases, that means we sold it, and received cash for it, cash increases)
- Add any *increases* in current liabilities (for example, if you purchase items on credit and your accounts payable increases, you did not need to use cash, so accounts payable are a source of funds, cash increases)
- Subtract any *decreases* in current liabilities (again, if your accounts payable balance were to go down, it would be because you paid it off with cash, cash decreases)

Cash flows from investing activities include any purchase or sale of securities (like stocks or bonds) that are not the company's own securities. So if you are ABC Co., and you buy or sell XYZ, Inc. stock, that would qualify as an investing activity. Additionally, the purchase or sale of property, plant, and equipment would be considered an investing activity.

Cash flows from financing activities would include the buyback—repurchase or issuance (sale)—of securities of the company itself. If ABC Co. issues ABC stock, that would be considered a source of funding. If the company repurchases stocks, retires bonds, or pays out dividends, those are all considered uses of cash from financing activities.

Once you have determined all the sources and uses of funds from the three different types of activities, they can be combined into one statement and used to arrive at a total increase or decrease in cash for the time period being measured.

SECTION 1.5: STATEMENT OF OWNER'S EQUITY

The final statement we will review is the statement of owner's equity, which shows the changes in the amount of equity (ownership) in the company over a specific period of time. It is generally the shortest financial statement, because there are only two types of transactions to record.

Specifically, that would be any gains in the form of net profit or owner's contributions, or any losses in the form of net loss or owner's withdrawals during the same time period.

The statement can be expressed in the following equation:

Beginning Capital Balance
+ Income earned
+ Owner's contributions
- Losses incurred
- Owner's withdrawals

= Ending Capital Balance

One key benefit of the statement of owner's equity is the ability for outside users of the financial statements to determine how much of a change in equity was due to the success of business operations versus owner's contributions of money to keep a business running. For example, start-ups are likely going to see less income and more contributed capital in the early stages of funding their business. For more established businesses, it should generally be the opposite: more net income, less contributed capital.

Section 2.1: Ratio Analysis

Financial ratio analysis is a method of using numbers from the above-referenced financial statements in order to measure and evaluate the financial performance of a firm or industry in a wide variety of ways. We will be looking at key metric areas such as liquidity, solvency, market prospects, profitability, and more.

It is worth noting that many key financial ratios can be found on popular financial news websites such as Yahoo!, and there are many other companies who provide financial services such as Standard & Poor's. Internet research is a ubiquitous and valuable tool to today's financial statement and ratio users. Information about any publicly traded company is usually just a few clicks away. Additionally, most large companies will have an "investor relations" section on their corporate websites that will contain all financial documents, which are often available for free download.

SECTION 2.2: LIQUIDITY RATIOS

Liquidity ratios measure how much cash or near-cash a company has on hand in order to meet their short-term obligations such as interest payments or accounts payable. The two most common liquidity ratios are the current ratio and the quick ratio.

The current ratio is a way to show how many current assets are available to pay back current liabilities. Generally, the higher the ratio, the better, because it means there are more current assets than short-term debt obligations to cover. This ratio is one of the most used to assess the financial health of a company. If they cannot meet their current obligations, that is a clear sign they are in trouble. If they can meet their current obligations, chances are good this will continue and carry over into their longer-term obligations. Think of it as if you are analyzing any individual's finances. If they are paying all their bills on a monthly basis, you have good reason to believe that five years from now, they will have the ability to do the same.

Current Ratio = Current Assets / Current Liabilities

The quick ratio (sometimes known as the acid test ratio) takes inventory out of the equation due to the fact that inventory may not be as liquid, and is sometimes sold on credit, rather than cash, so it is not a reliable indicator of liquidity. The higher the ratio, the better, but even a ratio that is less than one (meaning they have fewer "quick assets" than current liabilities) doesn't mean they are not financially stable. It could mean, however, that they are too heavily invested in inventory and that level should change in order to alleviate the strain on the quick ratio and ensure there are enough liquid assets available at all times to meet current obligations.

Quick ratio = (Current Assets – Inventory) / Current Liabilities

SECTION 2.3: SOLVENCY

Solvency ratios are similar to liquidity ratios in that they are a measure of a company's ability to pay off debts, but instead of focusing solely on the short-term, these measures help assess the long-term prospects of a company's ability to pay off their debt. This is done by looking at debt, assets, and equity in a variety of ways. We will look at six common solvency ratios: the debt ratio, the equity ratio, the debt to equity ratio, times interest earned, fixed charge coverage, and a ratio known as the solvency ratio. Some of the names of these ratios sound very similar, so it's important to understand the differences between them.

The debt ratio shows the percentage of the firm's assets financed by debt, both short-term and long-term. The higher this ratio, the more debt a company has, the more fixed obligations it has committed to, and therefore, their risk level increases.

Debt Ratio = Total Debt / Total Assets

The higher this ratio, in general, the better it is for a company. The reason is that equity financing is usually going to be a less expensive option for a company, and it does not lock them into long-term fixed obligations like debt does with its interest expense.

Equity Ratio = Total Equity / Total Assets

This ratio shows the proportion of debt to equity, and in general, the lower this number, the more solvent the company is.

Debt to Equity Ratio = Total Debt / Total Equity

This ratio shows how many times earnings before interest and taxes will cover all interest expenses, and the higher it is, the more solvent a company is, because they have enough income to cover expenses.

Times interest earned = EBIT / Interest

This ratio is similar to times interest earned, only it is a bit more of a conservative measure, because it will include items like leases, which are often long-term in nature, just like interest expenses.

Fixed charge coverage = Earnings before fixed charges and taxes / Fixed charges

As mentioned above, the solvency ratio is another way to assess solvency by using after-tax income and adding back depreciation for cash flow purposes. This measure is more conservative because it deals strictly with cash flows (which, as we learned above, may not always correspond to when revenue is recognized).

Solvency ratio = Net income plus depreciation / Total Debt

SECTION 2.4: MARKET PROSPECT RATIOS

Market prospect ratios are those you are probably already familiar with hearing in financial news reports, even if you are not yet sure what they are referring to. These are ratios such as earnings per share (EPS), price-to-earnings ratio (PE), dividend payout ratio (DPR), and dividend yield. These ratios measure the performance of a company's stock as it is traded in the stock market. These ratios are very useful for comparing a company's performance over time, and are a way to standardize stock performance and compare to other companies in the same industry and the industry as a whole.

If you think back to the bottom line of our income statement, you will remember net income, and that this money is what is left over for stockholders. When you divide this total number by all the shares the company has issued publicly (often referred to as common shares outstanding), you get the earnings per share figure. The higher this number, generally, the more profitable a company is. However, there are ways to inflate EPS through accounting conventions, or by buying back a large number of shares in the market, so it is important to always view EPS against other measures and never rely solely on this measure when making a stock pick.

EPS = Net Income / Shares Outstanding

The PE Ratio is one of the most commonly referenced ratios in the financial news and among analysts when deciding which stocks to choose. This is because the PE ratio essentially standardizes the price of any stock in terms of how much investors are currently willing to pay to get $1 of earnings for any particular stock. For example a PE of 15 means an investor is willing to pay $15 to earn $1. Another stock in the same industry might have a PE of $30. If investors are willing to pay $30 for the benefit of $1 in earnings, it could be an indication they expect those earnings to rise. But this interpretation should be taken lightly. It could also simply mean the second stock is far too expensive, and you should probably just buy the first stock instead, because you still get $1 of earnings for 50% less cost! If you feel confused about the PE ratio, do not worry, it is much more open to interpretation than many in the finance industry would lead you to believe. The rule of thumb is, the higher the PE, the better the stock (although this is not always true). Additionally, this number can be changed with accounting techniques, so it must be viewed in context with other measures.

PE Ratio = Stock Price per share / Earnings per share

The next ratio, dividend payout ratio, simply shows what percentage of earnings are paid out to investors in the form of cash dividends. Unlike other ratios, where we are looking for high or low numbers, investors tend to want to see a consistent number over time, one that is predictable, such as growing at a consistent rate, and not one that is trending lower over time. So, if the dividend payout ratio is high, investors want it to stay that way. Similarly, if the dividend payout ratio is low, that can also be acceptable to investors depending on the industry, but again, they want that ratio to stay stable. Stable dividends tend to signal to investors the company is also stable financially. But yet again, we have to be careful with this metric, as there have been cases where companies go so far as to borrow funds just to maintain a stable dividend, which would actually increase their debt, risk, and reduce their solvency—none of those things are good for stability.

DPR = Total Dividends / Net Income

The dividend yield is the percentage of a stock's return due to dividends. This is important because total returns from a stock are made up of stock appreciation (the increase in value over a period of time) and any dividend paid out. In general, a higher dividend ratio is desirable, because it means more cash flow to an investor. But this depends on each investor, their dividend preferences, and their personal tax and investing situation.

Dividend yield = Cash dividends per share / Price per share

SECTION 2.5: PROFITABILITY AND DUPONT SYSTEM OF ANALYSIS

The profitability ratios of a company are some of the most important to know and understand, because they reveal the ways the company achieves profits using assets, debt, and equity. Generally speaking, the higher the profitability ratio, the more positive it is for the company. Common profitability ratios include (net) profit margin, return on assets (ROA), and return on equity (ROE). We will also be looking at the DuPont system of analysis, which is a methodology to analyze the factors that lead to higher profits through the combination of specific ratios.

(Net) Profit margin = Net Income / Total Sales

While there are several levels of profit on the income statement that can all be measured by creating a ratio, the most often used ratio is net profit margin, because it is the bottom line earnings of the corporation after all expenses are considered.

Return on Assets = Net Income / Total Assets

As a company grows, so does their investment in total assets, which in turn is deployed to generate sales. In theory, the more assets a company owns, the more they should be able to use those assets to generate sales, and ultimately, profits. Return on assets is a measure of how good a company's assets are at generating profits. Another way to look at it is for every dollar of assets, how much in profit can be made.

Return on Equity = Net Income / Stockholder's Equity

Return on equity is a measure of how well stockholder investments generate profits for the company. Similar to ROA, ROE measures how much profit one dollar of equity can generate.

DuPont ROA = Profit Margin x Total Asset Turnover

Note: Profit Margin = Net Income / Sales; Total Asset Turnover = Sales / Total Assets

The DuPont system of analysis was actually created by the DuPont Corporation, and they championed the idea that return on assets can be achieved by one of two ways, or a combination of two ways. Specifically, a company could be very good at generating a high profit margin, usually by enjoying a high sales price and low relative costs. An example could be a luxury watch manufacturer, who sells their watches for a high price and fewer units. Alternatively, a company could turn over assets (such as inventory) at a very high rate, even with low profit margins, and still generate a high return on assets. To contrast with the luxury watch maker, a consumer watch maker with a reasonable price point who sells many more watches at a lower price point could still be just as profitable. It is easy to see how a mid-level watch manufacturer could have some combination of profits and turnover and also enjoy a high level of return on assets.

DuPont ROE = ROA / 1 – (Debt / Assets)

As can be seen from the DuPont ROE equation, a higher return on equity could be caused by a higher return on assets (we just learned the two factors that affect ROA above), or a higher use of debt in the capital structure (the capital structure is how a company is financed.) That is, the greater the debt, the greater the return on equity. However, it is important to note that just because more debt leads to greater return on equity, does not mean greater debt is preferable. Too much debt in the capital structure is still negative for the reasons mentioned in the above discussion of solvency ratios.

Section 3.1: Taxes

Entire courses could be written on the subject of personal and corporate taxation, but we are going to keep things simple for the purposes of this text. Return again to the income statement and recall that once we have determined earnings after accounting for interest expenses, we arrive at EBT, or earnings before taxes. It is *this* earnings figure, after COGS and all operating expenses and interest have been subtracted from revenues, that we apply our corporate tax rate (which can change on an annual basis, so always ensure you have proper estimates when budgeting for taxes).

SECTION 3.2: AVERAGE VS. MARGINAL TAX RATES

For a household or business, average and marginal tax rates must be known. The average tax rate is calculated as the total tax a company pays divided by the taxable income. For example, if a household earns $50,000 and they pay $7,000 in taxes, their average tax rate is $7,000 divided by $50,000, or 14%. Similarly, if a company pays $20,000 in taxes and their taxable income is $100,000, their average tax rate is 20%. This is a straightforward calculation.

Marginal tax rates are different, and relate to the concept of a tax schedule, which is produced each year by the IRS and is a list of how much certain levels of personal or corporate income are taxed in a given year. For example, in 2017, if a business earned $50,000, they would be taxed at 15%. However, every dollar after $50,000 and up to $75,000 is taxed at a rate of 25%.

This is the marginal tax rate—the tax rate applied to the last dollar of income. The reason it is important is because many people and companies may actually find attempting to earn past $50,000 discouraging, because they are taxed at a rate of 10% more for higher earnings, which can feel like a disincentive. Please note, marginal and corporate tax rates are subject to change, and the information provided here should be checked at IRS.gov or with the appropriate tax professional before acting upon it.

SECTION 3.3: CORPORATE TAX

One aspect of taxation that applies to business owners that is not a benefit to personal households is the concept of depreciation. We mentioned depreciation in the financial statements section (income statement and statement of cash flows) but you may not know what it is referring to.

Depreciation is a tax benefit where the value associated with the purchase of property, plant, or equipment can be deducted from taxable income over time. If you recall on the income statement, depreciation as a line item is deducted along with selling, general, and administrative expenses. This reduces the amount of income available to be taxed, and we also refer to this as an "above the line" deduction.

Let's look at an example. Two companies, Firm A and Firm B, have the same revenues of $200,000, COGS of $50,000, SG&A of $25,000, but Firm B has $20,000 in depreciation expense (sometimes called depreciation allowance), while Firm A has no depreciation expense. If both are taxed at a 25% corporate tax rate, what is the difference in taxes that they have to pay?

We can solve this by creating two income statements, side by side.

	Firm A	**Firm B**
Sales	$200,000	$200,000
COGS	$50,000	$50,000
Op. Profit	$150,000	$150,000
SG&A	$25,000	$25,000
Depreciation	$0	$20,000
EBIT	$125,000	$105,000
Taxes (25%)	$31,250	$26,250

As you can see, Firm A has to pay $31,250 in taxes, and Firm B's taxes are lower, $26,250. Firm B is paying $5,000 less in taxes due to the depreciation allowance.

Section 4.1: Time Value of Money

Time value of money is one of the central concepts in personal and business finance. The official definition you will read in most finance textbooks is that the time value of money is the concept that "money you have today is worth more than the same amount of money received in the future." Now, this textbook definition doesn't explain *why* that is the case. If you think about it, why would getting $5,000 be worth more than getting it tomorrow, or in a week, or in a year? Isn't $5,000 always worth $5,000?

This is a false statement for two reasons. First of all, if you were given $5,000 today, and simply placed it under a mattress for a year, you might think your money was very safe, and you still have $5,000, right? Technically you do, in *nominal* terms. (Nominal means in name only, so you are calling what you have "$100" but it is not worth what it was when you first obtained it.) In terms of real value, in terms of buying power, that $5,000 is worth less because of inflation and opportunity cost.

Inflation is the gradual erosion of the value of money over time due to the general increase in prices of goods and services. You only have to think about how cereal used to cost around $2 dollars per box, and today it can be around $4-5 dollars per box to understand inflation. Opportunity cost is the loss associated with the time value of money, because you could have done something productive with the money over time. The time value of money is the idea that due to the nature of compound interest, when we deploy our money for productive uses, we can dramatically increase our earnings over time. It is well known that time is one of the most important assets a person has, and that is why it is so important to understand how we grow money over time.

So what are the productive uses of money, and how do we know they are productive? Instead of putting $5,000 under a mattress, you could put it into an interest bearing savings account. This is a better option, but still holds potential to lose money if the interest rate isn't keeping pace with inflation. Another option is to invest in the stock market. This holds great promise of higher returns, but also much higher risk. Still another option is to invest your money in some kind of business or project of your own which you believe will make more money. Again, there is some level of risk and reward to consider.

So, what can be done? If each option has some potential to lose or gain money over time, how do you make a decision? Well, that is where time value of money calculations come in to aid in your decision-making. But just know your results are only going to be as good as your estimates, so time value of money calculations are not some kind of promise of earnings, but general guidelines so you can make better decisions.

Let's look at our $5,000 investment options in greater detail. Let's say we want to try to put it into a savings account where we earn simple interest of 2% annually over the next ten years. Simple interest is just taking the principal lump sum ($5,000) and applying an interest rate to it, and adding up the interest over ten years:

($5,000 x 2%) x 10 = $1,000 in interest

You can earn $100 per year, and over ten years that will add up to $1,000. That doesn't seem too bad! But what if you are earning *compound* interest? This is where the magic of time value of money comes in. Let's see what happens to the same amount of money and interest earned.

Year 1: $5,000 x 2% = $100.00
Year 2: $5,100 x 2% = $102.00
Year 3: $5,202 x 2% = $104.04
Year 4: $5,306.04 x 2% = $106.12
Year 5: $5,412.16 x 2% = $108.24
Year 6: $5,520.40 x 2% = $110.41

Year 7: $5,630.81 x 2% =	$112.62
Year 8: $5,743.43 x 2% =	$114.87
Year 9: $5,858.30 x 2% =	$117.17
Year 10: $5,975.47 x 2% =	$119.51
Total =	$1,094.98

As you can see, we earn almost $100.00 in additional interest when we have the benefit of compound interest, nearly one full year's worth of additional interest over when we invested using simple interest. This is the power of compound interest and time value of money.

The downside to this approach is that it would take a very long time to calculate anything if we had to use this long form to do so. Luckily there are formulas as well as calculators we can use to calculate time value of money much more easily. For the purposes of this text we will be using the TI BA II Plus, which can be purchased online or even downloaded as an app if you have a smartphone. Other financial calculators can also be used, just know you may need to refer to the user's manual to learn the different keystrokes to solve the problem, as they may be slightly different from what you are shown here.

If you have the calculator, please locate the row of gray buttons three rows down from the top. They are going to be labeled: N, I/Y, PV, PMT, and FV and you will learn what these numbers mean as we continue. For now just locate them. You will also need to know the compute button (CPT), located in the top left most corner of the calculator, as well as 2ND, the yellow button just below CPT, and then CE/C at the very lower left corner.

Now that you have located these buttons, you are ready to turn on and set up your calculator. It is also recommended, for the purpose of this text, to set your compounding periods per year to one period only. When you first get the calculator, the default setting is for compounding to occur twelve times per year, or monthly. You will soon understand why this default is not helpful for solving the problems in this section. So please press 2ND, then I/Y, and then the number 1. Next, press ENTER, then 2ND, and finally CPT. This will return you to a blank screen and you will be ready for the time value of money calculations we do later.

Additionally, it is recommended to set your decimal places to at least four spaces. This is a common convention when doing financial calculations, and will help reduce the instance of incorrect answers due to rounding discrepancies. To change the number of decimal places, you will press 2ND, then the decimal button. You will be prompted to enter a number, and press the number 4. Then press ENTER, which will lock in your choice.

Now let's return to our $5,000 investment problem. Above we solved this the long way. Using a financial calculator will save time. In order to solve this very same problem on a financial calculator, we need to categorize the different variables as follows and enter by pressing the number first, followed by the button:

$5,000 = PV (Present Value)
10 = N (Number of Years)
2 = I/Y (Interest Rate) Note: We enter this as a whole integer, never as the decimal form.

These are the only variables provided in our word problem, so now that they are entered, we can solve for the future value, or the total amount we will receive in the future, by pressing CPT and then FV. The following number should be displayed: -$6,094.97.

Another important thing to notice is that the negative sign in front of the answer does *not* mean a negative return or negative value. In other words, you did not lose $6,094.97. The negative sign simply represents a cash flow, and in this case, a negative sign stands for an *outflow of funds*. In this example, the outflow is out of the savings account where you kept the money for ten years. Notice that in our original problem we entered our $5,000 as a positive cash flow, which represented an inflow into the savings account. By entering 10, we told the financial calculator we wanted to invest for ten years, so it works under the assumption we would withdraw the funds after ten years, and hence, the negative cash flow sign.

Let's get back to our answer of, $6,094.97. Notice it is the same amount of interest we calculated when we used the long form to solve the problem: $5,000 + $1,094.98 = $6,094.98. You may also notice the numbers are off by one cent. This is common when doing these types of calculations by hand versus using a financial calculator. (As a side note, if you are taking a quiz or exam with multiple-choice options and the answers are off by a few cents or a few dollars, that is generally nothing to worry about and is simply due to the effects of rounding differences.)

Now that you have had a solid introduction to the concepts of simple and compound interest, as well as how to calculate a future value using the calculator, let's look at more examples.

SECTION 4.2: PRESENT VALUE (LUMP SUM AND ANNUITY)

When you see the term *present value lump sum*, you should know you are being asked to find the present value of a lump sum *to be received at some point in the future*. For example, if you know you will receive $10,000 at some point in the future (a future lump sum), you may wish to determine the *present value lump sum* that you started with. Using this example, let's say you will have $10,000 in five years, at an interest rate of 10%. How much money do you need to start with (the present value lump sum) to get to that $10,000?

Let's set up our variables. It is always recommended that you write down your variables as shown below every time you approach a new time value of money problem. This is part of the habit and discipline of accurate record keeping that is valuable in all areas of finance. Writing down your variables in an orderly way will help reduce any keystroke errors by visually organizing your work. Building a habit of consistent record keeping is a skill every financial professional must have.

$10,000 = FV
10 = I/Y
5 = N
CPT
PV = ? = $6,209.21

You will need $6,209.21 today (present value) in order to earn $10,000 in five years at 10% compound interest. As you can see, the power of compound interest is considerable, but 10% is also a rather high rate of return, so it is important to be realistic when you are using rates of return in your own calculations.

Let's use another example. Suppose that five years from now, you want to take a vacation. You know the resort in the Bahamas and an all-inclusive package at a five-star establishment will cost you $8,000. You also saw your local bank advertise high-interest savings accounts earning 4% compound interest. You are curious if the $4,000 you have today will be enough to reach $8,000 in five years. Is it?

To solve this, we write down our known variables:

$8,000 = FV
5 = N
4 = I/Y
CPT
PV = ? = $6,575.42

Unfortunately, no. You would end up with $6,575.42. Therefore, you will need to come up with an additional $2,575.42 if you want to have the $8,000 you need in five years for this trip. Did you notice how including the $4,000 in the story problem may have thrown you off? Did you want to include this number as a PV, and then weren't sure where to go? Be vigilant as you read these story problems to ensure you are able to pick out only the information pertinent to solving the problem at hand. You will get better at this over time and with lots of practice.

So far we have only considered lump sum investments. What if we have an equal sized payment that we deposit every year? For example, let's say we know we can afford to invest $1,000 every year for the next five years. We would call this an *annuity*, which is a series of equal payments at regular intervals over time. Examples of annuities would be things like a preferred stock investment that pays a set dividend amount every quarter. Another example would be a lottery winner who receives the equivalent of $1 million dollars by receiving equal payments of $100,000 over ten years' time.

Another example of an annuity might be if you are interested in buying a car, and you know that you can afford to pay $5,000 toward the price of the car every year for the next four years, on a loan with an interest rate of 6%. What is the present value of the price of the car you can afford today?

In order to solve this problem, we will be using the PMT button in our variables as we set up our problem, rather than FV or PV, which are both indicative of lump sums. This is because PMT indicates a payment that occurs every time period as entered into the financial calculator, and this button will automatically take into consideration that the payment occurs every year. In other words, you simply enter the equal payment amount one time, and the calculator knows to include that value on an annual basis for the total number of years you input into the N variable.

$5,000 = PMT
4 = N
6 = I/Y
CPT
PV = ? = $17,325.53

We can see that we could afford a car that costs approximately $17,300 today with a loan that has a 6% annual interest rate.

One benefit of using a financial calculator to solve time value of money problems is you can solve for other variables as long as you have the right information. For example, we have been looking at the present value of an annuity type problem. What if we know the present value, but want to solve for the payment amount instead? It is as simple as pressing the payment button to solve. Let's look at an example.

Let's say you have $10,000 today. You want to start a bakery and you know the rent will cost you $2,000 per year. If you are earning 5% in a savings account and you know you will need five years to run the business before it is profitable (meaning, you only have the $10,000 to rely on to pay for the bakery for the next five years), can you do it?

$10,000 = PV
5 = N
5 = I/Y
CPT
PMT = ? = \$2,309.75

Yes, you will have more than enough to afford the annual rent of $2,000 for five years.

SECTION 4.3: FUTURE VALUE (LUMP SUM AND ANNUITY)

In the introduction to this section, we actually discussed the *future value of a lump sum*, although you may not have realized it yet. Simply put, we took a sum today (the present value) and looked at how much money we would get in the future at a specific interest rate, compounded, over a specific period of time. The procedure is very similar to what we have done so far, and the only real difficulty students encounter is in the interpretation of the time value of money story problems. So let's get some additional practice.

If you have $5,000 today and you know you can invest in a very exciting new project that will guarantee returns of 25% over the next ten years, what amount of dollar return can you expect to enjoy in the future?

(As a side note, a rate of return of 25% is highly remarkable, and is not likely to be found in many opportunities these days unless they are also equally risky!)

$5,000 = PV
10 = N
25 = I/Y
CPT
FV = ? = \$46,566.13

Suppose you plan to purchase a new home in five years. You believe that home will cost you $250,000 and your goal is to pay 100% cash upfront because you really dislike debt. You currently have $100,000 saved up today and believe you can earn 5.75% during that time. Will you have enough money?

$100,000 = PV
5 = N
5.75 = I/Y
CPT
FV = ? = \$132,251.88

No, you are not even close to the amount you are going to need. This is very frustrating to you and you decide you still want this house and are going to take on an extra job to find the money to pay for it. How much more money would you need to earn each year in order to make $250,000?

This additional question added to the original problem requires you to synthesize some information from the previous work you did and think critically about how to solve using time value of money solutions.

First, you need to determine how much more money you would need in the future by looking at how much you need versus how much you are currently projected to receive at the end of five years:

$250,000 - $132,251.88 = $117,748.12

So this $117,748.12 represents the amount of money you need to come up with in five years, and you plan to work in order to earn it. So how do we figure out how much per year you need to earn? Just like in the previous section, we can also solve for an annuity. Here we can turn that $117,748.12 into a future value amount and solve for the annuity or payment of a future value.

$117,748.12 = FV
5 = N
5.75 = I/Y
CPT
PMT = ? = $20,992.62

You can see that you would need a job that pays you an extra $20,992.62 per year in order to afford the house, in addition to the $100,000 you already have. Of course, this problem assumes you are purchasing the entire house upfront for cash, which is not usually the case for most homebuyers. But it should be clear that you could use time value of money calculations to find solutions to some difficult financial situations.

In the above annuity problem we solved for the PMT. Let's look at another future value of an annuity type problem, where we know the PMT but we need to find the FV. Let's say you are planning on earning $800 a year for the next six years from a side business, with the ultimate goal of buying a new motorcycle that is going to cost you $5,000. Will you earn enough to make your goal if you think you can earn 10% per year?

$800 = PMT
6 = N
10 = I/Y
CPT
FV = ? = $6,172.49

Yes, you will earn enough money.

SECTION 4.4: ANNUITY DUE VERSUS ORDINARY ANNUITY

Now that you have mastered the basics of time value of money using your financial calculator, let's add another concept and function on your calculator. In all the annuity problems we have worked on so far, whether you knew it or not, the assumption the calculator was working with was that all payments were occurring at the end of each time period, which, for our purposes, is one year. When payments occur at the end of a time period, it is known as an *ordinary annuity*.

There is another type of annuity called an *annuity due*, which is where payments occur at the beginning of a time period. (This can be a confusing point for students, because the word "due" seems to indicate a time in the future and many students think of this as the end of something.) If you can remember an annuity due is similar to any kind of regular payment you make that is due each month (usually at the *beginning* of each month, such as rent or tuition payments), you can hopefully remember annuity due has to do with beginnings.

Both ordinary annuity and annuity due still have the same basic feature in common: both pay an equal amount over a fixed interval of time. The only difference is *when* that timing occurs—at the beginning (annuity due) or end (ordinary annuity) of a time period.

Now, the reason timing is so important is that it will significantly change how much money can be earned during the same period of time. If you think about it logically, payments that occur at the beginning of a time period have much more time to earn interest than do those that are made at the end of a time period. The best way to illustrate this point is with examples, but first you need to learn how to make the annuity due versus ordinary annuity changes on your calculator.

First, let's identify the BGN function on our calculator. If you look just above the row of grey buttons, you will see that each button has small yellow letters. These letters will be active when you press the yellow 2ND button. So, if you press 2ND and then PMT, you will see the word END on the screen. Next, press 2ND and ENTER, which will activate the BGN function on the calculator. Go ahead and try it now. After you press these buttons in sequence, you should see small BGN letters in the upper right hand corner of your calculator screen. If you don't see the letters, it means the calculator is still in END mode and you *will get the wrong answers*. Repeat the sequence above to ensure you see the small BGN in the upper right corner. While in BGN mode, you will complete your annuity problem as we did in the above sections and the calculator will automatically change the timing of the cash flows for you. This is important to understand because once you have completed any annuity due problem, you will want to ensure you change back out of BGN mode right away so that other problems you calculate are not done in the wrong mode. To change back to END mode you will press 2ND, PMT, 2ND, and then ENTER. When the small BGN disappears, you are all set.

Now, let's look at how the use of an annuity due versus an ordinary annuity affects the final results of a calculation.

Let's say you have $1,000 to invest each year for the next twenty years. If you can earn 4% interest, how much will you earn if you invest at the beginning of the year (annuity due), versus if you invest at the end of the year (ordinary annuity)?

	Annuity Due	**Ordinary Annuity**
PMT =	$1,000	$1,000
N =	20	20
I/Y =	4	4
	BEGIN Mode	END Mode
FV =	$30,969.20	$29,778.08

As you can see, we earn more money with the annuity due, even though we have invested the same amount of money over the same number of years at the same interest rate. What has made the difference of $30,969.20 - $29,778.08 = $1,191.13? That extra year of time we gain by starting our investment today and investing for twenty years rather than investing one year from today and investing for the same twenty years. If you think about it, with an ordinary annuity, our final payment in year twenty does not get the benefit of compound interest at all. Therefore, when all variables are equal, we can automatically conclude that the annuity due will be worth more.

Let's look at another example.

You have asked your sister if you can rent out space above her garage in order to start a candle-making business. She says you are welcome to do so, but must pay her on the first of each year for the next five years, or until you can afford your own workshop. You agree to pay her $200 per month, paid in full each year. If interest rates are 3%, what is the value of this agreement five years from now?

BGN Mode
PMT = $200 x 12 = $2,400
N = 5
I/Y = 3
FV = ? = $13,124.18

Did you catch the tricky part of this word problem? The $200 was a *monthly* figure, but must be paid in full each year, so that is really $200 x 12 = $2,400. Did you also make sure your calculator was in BGN mode? Make sure you really take your time reading these story problems and ensure you write all variables down before you go about solving problems.

Section 5.1: Interest Rate Calculations

In the beginning of our discussion of the time value of money, we made a distinction between simple interest and compound interest. If you recall, simple interest is earned only on a principal amount. While compound interest is earned on the principal and then as interest accrues and is added to the original balance, the new interest accrues on the principal plus interest balance, which leads to exponential growth over long periods of time.

Up until this point we have assumed annual compounding for the sake of simplicity. In reality, however, compounding can actually occur over smaller time periods: quarterly, monthly, weekly, daily, or even continuously.

There are interest rate calculations we will look at in this text: the equivalent annual rate, which is also known as the effective annual rate and considers compounding, and the annual percentage rate, which considers simple interest. Let's look at both a bit more in-depth.

SECTION 5.2: EQUIVALENT ANNUAL RATE (EAR)

The equivalent annual rate or effective annual rate (EAR) is the rate that is required by law to be quoted whenever you are solicited by lenders such as banking institutions or credit cards. The reason is that unless a consumer knows the amount of interest they are really paying, they could be fooled into believing they are getting a lower rate than they really are, and paying more in interest than they originally anticipated.

This means that if you are depositing funds into a bank, you are going to be looking for a higher EAR because you will have the opportunity to earn more. However, the opposite is true if you were going to be borrowing. You would want a lower EAR, which would help keep your costs of borrowing low. But why is an EAR calculation necessary?

To use an example, let's assume the credit card rate you pay is compounded on a monthly basis. So if you were to get a credit card that said, "We charge 10%," but failed to mention they compound the interest on your remaining balance on a monthly basis, you might not realize you are actually paying more than 10%. How can that be?

We need to use the EAR formula, which is:

$$EAR = [(1 + r / n)\, ^\wedge n] - 1$$

Where:

r = stated interest rate

n = number of compounding periods; quarterly would equal 4, monthly would equal 12, etc.

Let's plug our 10% into this equation and see what we are really paying if it is compounded monthly.

EAR = [(1 + .10/12)^12] -1
EAR = [1.0083^12]-1
EAR = [1.1047]-1
EAR = .1047 or 10.47%

So you are really being charge 10.47% each year, not simply 10%. That extra 0.47% could really add up over time.

SECTION 5.3: ANNUALIZED PERCENTAGE RATE

As mentioned above, the annualized percentage rate, or APR, is a measure of simple interest. This is the rate we most often hear quoted in car commercials—"Get a new car with zero money down and 0% APR!" Usually there is a little asterisk next to that 0% APR, because car dealerships are not in the business of lending money for free! 0% APR offers are generally extended for an introductory period of time, until a regular APR kicks in.

So let's say you are buying a car, and you are offered 0% APR for the first six months of the year, but then it jumps to 1% APR per month after that. What do you think the annualized percentage rate will be? The calculation is simple, we just multiply the monthly rate by twelve months per year and get the APR. In this case 12 x 1% = 12%. In the United States there are laws about accurately disclosing any fees that you might also be paying, so this APR would be only if there are truly no other fees you need to pay.

Another example of APR is that a credit card company may advertise that they charge 1.5% APR, monthly. In order to determine the annual figure, again you just multiply by 12, to get 1.5% x 12 = 18%.

The other way APR is utilized is by including all the extra fees associated with any loan. To use an example, let's say you are planning to buy a house and your loan is for $150,000 at 4% APR. This would be known as the *nominal* interest rate, because it is the state rate we pay, but we are about to see that we really end up paying more, which is why the APR is so useful. The total interest you are paying on the home loan would be:

$150,000 x 4% = $6,000 per year interest

However, most home loans include many other fees, such as origination fees, insurance, and closing costs. Let's say this amounts to an additional $4,000 in fees. How can we determine the real APR?

First we add the $4,000 to the $150,000 loan and then we multiply *that* number by our APR again:

$154,000 x 4% = $6,160

Now we divide the new interest plus fees amount by the original loan amount to determine our real APR.

$6,160 / $150,000 = 4.11% APR

There is something called the Truth in Lending Act, which requires loan institutions to be upfront and disclose all the accurate costs to borrowers. However, there could be two institutions that offer the same nominal rate of 4%, but end up with different APRs. This could confuse borrowers who do not understand how an APR works. Let's look at one more example using our home loan scenario.

In the above example the lender had an additional $4,000 in fees. Now what if another lender offered the same interest rate, but had $3,500 in fees? How would that change the APR?

First we determine our new interest on the loan plus fees amount:

$153,500 x 4% = $6,140

Then we divide the new interest amount by the original loan amount:

$6,140 / $150,000 = 4.09%

As you can see, two lenders with the same nominal rate will end up quoting two different APRs, based on the extra fees involved in a loan.

One final word about interest rates and time value of money problems. When you are doing these practice problems, please note that the values are completely made up and may not have any relationship to the rates you can really find out in the market today. It would be a valuable exercise, however, to go online and do a bit of research as to what kinds of rates are common today, for things like lending for homes, small businesses, the average rates of return in the stock market over the last year, and last five years, so that as you perform these calculations, you can apply what you know to real world scenarios.

Section 6.1: Working Capital Management

In today's economy, businesses are growing faster than ever. It is often surprising for students of finance to learn that a business' rapid rise to success in the marketplace, in terms of demand for their products and services, can actually be one of the biggest reasons they fail. That might sound incredibly counterintuitive. Why would a company that enjoys considerable demand be at risk of failure? The answer is if they do not have the cash and current assets they need to meet demand.

Try to imagine a new company that sells the hottest new toy out there, let's call them Widget Spinners. The kids have gone crazy for Widget Spinners and the factory can barely keep up with demand. They are running low on inventory, and they have made many of their sales on credit to toy stores, bookstores, and retailers such as Target, such that they do not have the cash they need to purchase more inventory and they have maxed out the credit their suppliers are willing to extend (also known as trade credit). They are stuck in a terrible position unless they can infuse their business with more capital to keep it going, or they have to halt orders until receivables come in or more inventory is sold off, which would hurt their standing in the market and cause competitors to overtake them.

I hope this illustration shows how easy it would be for an up-and-coming company to completely fail as a victim of their own success and, more specifically, poor working capital management.

Working capital management is the financing and management of the current assets of the firm using short-term debt (such as current liabilities). Every single day, the current assets of a company are changing (at least, hopefully they are!) due to the receipt of cash from sales and accounts receivable, or cash going out to fund new inventory. There are decisions to be made on a daily basis about how much inventory your company should be holding at a given time—too much means you could run low on cash, too little means you could be missing crucial opportunities. Additionally, every growing business is going to need a source of short-term capital, and they will need to have access to it quickly.

Let's look at short-term sources of funding that are commonly used for working capital management.

SECTION 6.2: SHORT-TERM SOURCES OF FUNDS

The front line for sources of funds for the short-term needs of a business are those internally generated by inventory, which turn into sales and cash, and accounts receivable, which are credit sales that turn into cash. Sometimes accounts receivable do not convert to cash and these are called bad debts. This means we extended credit to someone who decided not to pay in full. A company clearly needs to minimize the amount of bad debt, and having a well-regulated credit and collections policy will be part of ensuring bad debts do not exceed a certain amount. Sometimes, even increasing staff or outsourcing to a company who focus solely on collections can increase the cash you receive.

As mentioned above, in the case of rapid growth, inventory and accounts receivable and payable may not realistically be able to fund all the future growth and increased inventory needs. This means the company will need to find external sources of funding. Various methods of funding (both internal and external) are listed below, and some are more desirable than others. This list is not exhaustive, but shows some of the variety of short-term funding options available.

Accounts payable stretching. This is essentially a way of self-funding by simply delaying payment to your suppliers, thereby extending the amount of time you have your own cash for use. This may be acceptable for a very short period of time, but it should never be relied upon as a regular strategy, or you risk alienating your suppliers who may in turn place your orders on lower priority or simply refuse to do business with you, viewing you as a credit risk. While *trade credit* is absolutely an acceptable form of funding short-term needs, it is best utilized by keeping on good terms and not relying too heavily on stretching payments, which can strain the relationship with your supplier.

Advances. Sometimes a customer may help fund short-term needs by paying in advance. A fairly new and popular example of this is the website Kickstarter, which requires interested customers to pay upfront for a product that has not been made yet, with the promise that they can be an early adopter if the funding goal is reached. Customer advances have been around as an inexpensive form of financing for businesses for a long time.

Commercial bank loan. For most businesses, obtaining a bank loan is a wise and simple choice, and bank loans represent the largest source of working capital for businesses in general. The funds can often be secured at a reasonable interest rate, called the prime loan, or prime plus some kind of premium based on the creditworthiness of the business. Sometimes the assets of the business are required as collateral.

Commercial paper. This is a way a corporation can get funding out in the market without having to register with the SEC, but it is only a viable option for very large, established, and credit-worthy companies. Usually, the principal plus interest due to investors must be repaid within 270 days.

Credit cards. Business credit cards can be used as a source of short-term funding, and may be the option many smaller businesses turn to, especially as they are just getting started in business. Of course, credit cards generally carry a high interest rate, so businesses should do their best not to carry a balance any longer than necessary.

Factoring. This method is when a company secures funding essentially by using their accounts receivable as collateral. This can be a very expensive method, but if you have plenty of accounts receivable that will come due in the near future, it might be a viable option.

Field warehouse financing. A lender will offer a loan with inventory held in the business' warehouse as collateral. The collateralized inventory must be physically separated and tracked. The lender will finance new raw materials for new inventory and be paid directly out of accounts receivable. This is a more costly method of borrowing.

Floor planning. This type of financing is common among retailers who need a loan to purchase high-priced inventory, such as cars, and the inventory itself is used as collateral. Borrowing fees are high, which is an incentive to sell the inventory as quickly as possible, which is why salespeople often work on commission in these types of high-priced retailers, in order to motivate the business to convert inventory to cash as soon as possible.

Line of credit. A line of credit is often a necessity for a business that regularly needs to draw down a loan amount, but can pay it back shortly. Sometimes collateral is required to be put up for the line of credit. The interest rate may be slightly higher than a conventional commercial loan.

As can be seen, there are many options for short-term funding for a business, and the options available depend largely on the operations of the firm and their creditworthiness.

SECTION 6.3: MANAGEMENT OF SHORT-TERM ASSETS AND LIABILITIES

The fixed assets of a firm tend to grow consistently over time, as the business reaches new levels of production. A growing business outgrows their current facility and needs a new one, so they fund the purchase of a warehouse with a long-term mortgage. This type of long-term planning happens over time and financial managers can often easily see the trajectory and need for funding long before the time to make the move arrives. However, short-term asset and liability management can be a bit more unpredictable and often requires fast decisions. How does a financial manager go about planning the inventory, accounts receivable and payable, and cash flows of the firm? This is where accurate forecasting and innovative inventory management systems are of critical importance.

SECTION 6.4: INVENTORY

How are levels of inventory to be determined? Every company should be making forecasts of product sales based on the past sales (if there are any) as well as expected demand based on many factors such as the type of product, if it is seasonal, what kind of competition is out there, etc. However, when there is a mismatch between projected sales and actual sales, there can either be a build-up of inventory or a reduction in inventory below levels that are appropriate to keep up with demand. Both situations are undesirable, because it means a mismanagement of funds and resources is occurring and needs to be corrected as quickly as possible.

For example, if you have ever gone to a store the day after a major holiday like Valentine's Day, you will often see big markdowns on the inventory they sold at full price just the day before. This is because they over-bought certain items, inaccurately estimating demand for, say, heart-shaped pillows, and they want to get these items out the door as soon as possible before they are completely worthless, so collecting 50-75% of their price is better than nothing. You might wonder, "Can't they just hold the inventory until next Valentine's Day and sell when demand is high again?" Yes, they could, but remember, there is also a cost associated with warehousing inventory. That is, keeping the products in storage until they are ready to sell. The cost of warehousing Valentine's pillows for an entire year might be more than the discounted price they can earn by selling now. As you can see, the decisions that need to be made have many factors to them, which is why working capital management requires quick, daily decisions to be successful as the market changes.

Every industry has to take into consideration their production cycle. For example, take a market such as cell phone manufacturers. They are constantly selling new product, but demand increases as a new version of their phone is released, and wanes as the product cycle dies down and competitor products with new technology are released. One can imagine the financial manager would need to secure a large amount of short-term funding for every product release and pay it down as inventory is sold off and hold less inventory of older versions as new ones are about to be released. This same pattern is true for all products where consumers expect upgrades.

What about products that never change, such as a company that makes the same red plastic cups for sale over and over? Those products still are likely to have seasonal increases in demand, such as during hot months when people are more likely to have outdoor parties and tailgating, and perhaps less demand in the colder months. But either way, they are likely to need to carry what are called "permanent" current assets, or inventory and receivables that maintain a rather consistent level over time, and then temporary growth in current assets on a seasonal basis.

There are two main ways to manage the production of inventory, just-in-time and level production. With just-in-time inventory management, the goal is to match demand and production as closely as possible, with no loss in demand due to customers not receiving their orders when they expect them. In today's economy, the ability to receive a desired item within several days or less, depending on the product, is a new expectation. The problem with just-in-time inventory is that the unpredictability of production can sometimes put a strain on equipment and labor that may need to suddenly ramp up production, or go through idle periods, both of which can lead to waste, missed opportunities, and unexpected costs. The solution might seem obvious: just produce a consistent amount of inventory over time, to keep production levels even and operate equipment and utilize labor at a consistent pace. However, this method might lead to build-ups in current assets that are undesirable, and the loss of cash and the need to find more funding due to lack of internally generated funds.

As you can see, understanding the life cycle of a product for a specific industry and how inventory demand may change over time is a very important first step in proper working capital management. Next we will look at the financial manager's decision in terms of managing accounts receivable.

SECTION 6.5: ACCOUNTS RECEIVABLE

Most businesses sell inventory by extending some portion of credit to their buyers. The level of accounts receivable build-up depends greatly on which method of production is chosen: just-in-time, or level production. As discussed above, both of these methods have implications for inventory levels, but that logically extends to levels of accounts receivable.

To understand this further, let's consider the cell phone manufacturer, whose product demand peaks every six months as new phone versions come out, and wanes as competitor products are released. In January and July, the production, as well as sales, for their products will peak. If they are selling a considerable amount of phones on credit, they will similarly experience a build-up in accounts receivable, which means their cash is tied up in receivables. Then, as sales decrease, the accounts receivable should be coming due. During those peaks is when the company is most likely to need short-term financing, but they should be able to pay it off fairly quickly when the receivables are converted to cash.

What if a company has level production and level sales? Going back to our red plastic cup manufacturer, they are less likely to experience a large build-up in inventory or receivables, and therefore their accounts receivable and collections should be fairly consistent and more likely to fund operations with internally generated cash and receivables.

SECTION 6.6: ACCOUNTS PAYABLE

So far, much of our discussion of working capital management has focused on cash, inventory, and receivables. We discussed trade credit and payables as a potential source of internally generated funds, but just as when a business sells and has terms for their receivables, the opposite is true of the company extending payables to a business.

Accounts payable management depends largely on good relationships with a business' suppliers. This means paying on time, paying in full, and demonstrating creditworthiness. Once a good relationship is established, a supplier may be willing to extend the trade credit terms, such as increasing the length of time a business can take to pay, and recognizing this is essentially an interest-free form of financing. Now, that does not mean there is no cost to extending payables. Trade terms often come with a form of a discount if cash is paid in full within a certain number of days. Therefore, while extending trade credit does not come with an interest rate, it does come with a cost, which is similar in nature.

Let's look at how trade credit terms often work.

A business can be offered credit terms of 2/10 net 30. What do each of these numbers mean? The 2 implies a 2% discount on the credit amount, and the 10 means the discount is available to the business for ten days (after the billing date). "Net 30" means that if the business does not pay within ten days, they must pay in full in thirty days, and they are no longer eligible to receive the 2% discount.

Let's see how this works with an actual dollar amount. If your business was extending $10,000 credit with terms 3/15 net 30, how much is the discount if they pay within fifteen days?

$10,000 x .97 = $9,700

They will receive a $300 discount if they pay early.

SECTION 6.7: SHORT-TERM INVESTMENTS

Up until this point, the discussion of working capital management has discussed the potential difficulties when a business is running low on cash and needs to find additional sources of income. However, some companies are in a position that they have excess cash, and they do not believe the best use is additional investment in inventory or even fixed assets. Instead of letting excess cash sit idle, these companies will augment their working capital strategy to leverage this cash to earn some extra interest using short-term (less than one year) investment strategies. In order for a short-term investment to be a good option, it must be highly liquid and convertible to cash in under one year. Therefore, any kind of security that is traded on major exchange, such as stocks and bonds, and has good trading volume, is a good choice.

You might be thinking that bonds are usually a long-term investment, and you are right, but if a bond is being sold that has less than one year to maturity, that can actually be considered a short-term investment. Additional options for short-term investments include commercial paper, which, as stated above, is a form of investment vehicle issued by large, creditworthy companies looking to finance their short-term obligations. Treasury bills also mature in less than 270 days and are highly sought-after forms of short-term financing because they are considered virtually risk-free and enjoy large trading volumes.

SECTION 6.8: CASH BUDGET

The cash budget is a forecasting tool that will allow a financial manager to anticipate the additional cash needs at any point in the future. Keep in mind that any forecasting tool is only as good as the inputs into it, and it should not be considered a crystal ball. A cash budget should be reviewed frequently and modified over time as cash and borrowing needs change.

Let's assume a business has determined it needs to keep $10,000 on hand to fund operations. We can assume that if their cash figure falls below $10,000, they will need to borrow the difference, and if it rises above $10,000, they can use that money to pay back any previously-borrowed funds. Let's see what this looks like with a sample cash budget over three months and cash flows.

	Month 1	Month 2	Month 3
Net cash flow	$1,000	($5,000)	$3,000
Beginning cash balance	$10,000	$11,000	$10,000
Cumulative cash balance	$11,000	$6,000	$13,000
Loan (Repayment)	$0	$4,000	($3,000)
Cumulative loan balance	$0	$4,000	$1,000
Ending cash balance	$11,000	$10,000	$10,000

As you can see here, in the first month, the company had a $10,000 cash balance, plus $1,000 in net cash flows, leaving them with $11,000 to start month two.

However, in month two they had negative $5,000 in cash flows, which dropped their cash balance below $10,000 to $6,000. This meant they needed to borrow $4,000 in short-term financing in order to maintain the $10,000 cash balance at the end of month two. In month three, they earned positive cash flows of $3,000, and because this increased their cash balance to $13,000, they were able to use $3,000 in order to pay down their debt to just $1,000 and still maintain a balance of $10,000 in cash. This should give you a better idea of the flow of cash versus borrowing in a company.

Section 7.1: Valuation and Characteristics of Stocks and Bonds

Valuation is a fundamental skill for any financial manager or investor. One of the most accepted definitions of valuation is, "the present value of all future cash flows of a business, investment, asset, or project discounted at an appropriate interest rate." We will see how this can be applied to stocks and bonds below, using what is known as a *discounting cash flow* model, because we take those future cash flows and discount them back to the present time. It will be important to recall the information we learned above in the time value of money section, because we are going to be building upon what we learned there. The idea that cash flows and interest rates can be used to determine a present value should feel familiar to you, and now we will expand those concepts and apply them to the ways businesses fund their companies.

Stocks and bonds are the main source of financing for the long-term needs of a company. As you will see, bonds are meant to be issued and held for many years, and similarly, stocks are often issued and held for many years as well. As long as the company is still operating, its stock can be traded in the market and stockholders can enjoy benefits such as capital appreciation (the rise in the price of the stock) and stock cash dividends (regular cash payments out of the earnings of the business).

However, the important aspect of valuation is determining the correct amount of future cash flows (which we have considered in our sections on the statement of cash flows and working capital management and the cash budget) as well as the required rate of return investors expect from an investment in the market. The required rate of return is determined by the risk-free rate plus any risk premiums for a particular investment, which is based on the economy in general, the industry of the company or company itself and its creditworthiness, and more.

The risk-free rate is really a theoretical figure, which is the return an investor will get on an investment that is zero risk, or in other words, the return you should expect on any investment as a baseline. From there, you are compensated additionally for the specific risk you encounter. Keep in mind there is no such thing as a truly risk free investment. Even though government securities are used as a proxy for the risk free rate because they are considered so safe since they are backed by the guarantees of sovereign governments who can simply print more money, it should be obvious this could lead to inflation, which can erode the value of currency. Additionally, governments are known to fail or decrease in their creditworthiness, especially in times of economic crisis, war, or other turmoil such as natural disasters.

SECTION 7.2: BONDS (VALUATION AND CHARACTERISTICS)

We have mentioned bonds, but let's look further at their characteristics and what kind of investment qualifies as a bond. First of all, a bond is a form of debt financing (a way of raising money for a business or project), that is issued (which is another term for being sold) by governments (federal, state, and municipalities can all sell forms of bonds) and corporations. Bonds are generally longer-term in nature, and take the form of contracts that promise a certain amount of interest as well as a principal amount to be repaid at a specified maturity date. The maturity date can be many years in the future, ten, twenty, and even in very rare cases, hundred-year bonds.

When an investor buys a bond, they usually pay an amount called the face value, which is generally set at $1,000 for a single bond. The bond will have a rate attached to it called a coupon rate, which is the amount of money the investor is contractually guaranteed to receive, usually semi-annually. For example, if a bond had a coupon rate of 8%, and it was paid semi-annually, the investor is owed $80, divided into two semi-annual payments, or $40.

The bond will also have another interest rate associated with it, called the yield to maturity. The yield to maturity is the theoretical rate of return an investor will earn if they purchase a bond and hold it until it matures, assuming all coupons and the final principal amounts are paid in full and on time.

It is extremely important students understand the difference between the coupon rate and the yield to maturity. These are two completely different rates with different meanings. It will be useful if a student can understand that a coupon is always associated with a dollar amount and when they see the term coupon, they should immediately think of changing the percentage into a dollar amount. Yield to maturity will always remain a pure interest rate.

This will become clearer if we apply these concepts to a time value of money problem where we value a bond. Thinking back to the time value of money section, we should immediately recognize that a bond is a combination of the two concepts we learned about: lump sum and annuity.

For the purposes of this text, the face value of a bond and its eventual principal payment are always equal to $1,000—this is the contractual obligation. The coupon payment represents an annuity, because it is always an equal amount (based on the coupon rate). As stated above, usually, bond coupon payments are paid semi-annually, but for our purposes we will assume they are paid annually for simplicity in solving our problems.

Imagine you just purchased a bond with $1,000 face value, which pays a coupon rate of 7%, has five years to maturity and is selling in the market at a yield to maturity of 8%. What is the present value of the bond?

Here is how we set up the variables:

FV = $1,000
PMT = $1,000 x .07 = $70*
N = 5
I/Y = 8
PV = ? = -$960.07

*Do you see how we immediately convert the percentage to a dollar amount?

There are some additional things you should know about bond valuation. First, note that the I/Y button is used for the yield to maturity figure, because the yield to maturity is the rate of return one can expect on the bond. Secondly, because there are two types of cash flows—principal amount and coupon payment—it is very important that you realize they need to have the same cash flow sign. As can be seen in the above problem, the face value or future value is a positive cash flow, as well as the coupon payment. This is because both those values will flow *to* the bondholder and *away from* the company that issued the bonds. These two values must always share the same cash flow sign. And finally, most bonds have a coupon and yield to maturity that are, by definition, equal at issuance. However, as time passes and the bond trades in the market, the coupon and yield to maturity can change, which then affects the price of the bond. In this example, as the yield to maturity increases over the coupon rate, the price of the bond decreases. The opposite would be true if the yield to maturity was 6%, but earning a 7% coupon, this would make the bond more valuable and command a higher price in the market.

SECTION 7.3: DEBENTURE

Now that we have reviewed some of the basic characteristics of bonds and how to value them, let's look at some of the different types of bonds and how they are issued. Debenture bonds are a common form of bond where the physical assets of the business are *not* used as collateral, but instead the general creditworthiness of the business is considered enough to invest in the bond. This type of bond is generally issued by very stable institutions like governments or very stable corporations, and are the most common form of debt financing. Just like most bonds (with the exception of zero coupon bonds which pay no coupon, but are offered at a deep discount), debenture bonds pay a set interest payment and bondholders are first in line for these payments prior to stockholders receiving dividend payments (which we discuss further, below).

Debentures can be further broken down into two types: convertible, and non-convertible. Non-convertible bonds are considered straight bonds that simply pay interest and principal at maturity, just as described above, whereas convertible bonds may have the option for the bondholder to convert the bonds into shares of corporate stock at some point. Adding a convertible feature can be a way to lower the interest rate on a bond, because some bondholders may wish to convert to stock if the stock is performing very well, and they enjoy having that option if they wish. The other benefit is if the stock is not performing well, the bondholder will still have the benefit of the consistent interest payment.

SECTION 7.4: SINKING FUNDS

A sinking fund is sometimes attached to a bond issue in order to increase the creditworthiness of the offering, thereby reducing the interest rate the company needs to pay. The sinking fund is essentially a pool of money set aside to buy back the bond issue over time, which increases the chances the remaining bondholders are paid on time and in full, and reduces the risk of default, which in turn reduces the risk of investing in the bond offering.

How does a sinking fund work? A separate account, called a custodial account, is set up and is run by a trustee. A trustee is an organization or person who is given legal power over the funds in the account and they are required to use the funds to pay down the debt by retiring it early. Retiring essentially means paying off current bondholders and taking some of the bonds out of circulation completely. This reduces the amount of interest payments the company is obligated to pay over the life of the bonds. Cash, stocks, and even other bonds can fund sinking funds, but payment might not be made into the account right away, which is logical because if the company had the cash to do so, they probably would not have needed to issue bonds in the first place.

SECTION 7.5: COUPON

A coupon bond is basically what we have described up until this point, a bond that promised a certain interest payment, also called the coupon payment, at set intervals over the life of the bond. Coupon bonds used to actually be issued as a small booklet with paper coupons, which a bondholder had to turn in as proof of ownership to receive their interest payment. Today electronic record keeping ensures that bondholders' information is properly stored and coupons are automatically paid to the proper entity, on time.

It is important to realize that the value of a coupon for any particular bond will change over time as the bond is traded on the open market and its value changes. To understand this, let's look at an example.

As mentioned, when a bond is issued, the coupon rate and the yield to maturity are the same. That is because a 7% coupon bond being sold for $1,000 is going to yield 7% return to maturity.

$70 / $1,000 = 7%

But what about a 7% coupon bond that sells for $900? What happens to the coupon yield (the rate of return of the coupon payment itself)?

Divide the coupon payment by the new value:

$70 / $900 = 7.78%

As you can see, the same coupon amount, $70, is yielding a higher rate of return because the price of the bond went down. We could also infer the yield to maturity increased, because we know there is an inverse relationship between bond prices and bond yields.

SECTION 7.6: COMMON STOCK AND PREFERRED STOCK

When discussing characteristics of equity and valuation, it is often common to consider that the value of a share of stock is the present value of the future dividends to be received. The dividends in this case are the cash flows of the stock.

There are essentially three different ways a company rewards its stockholders:

1. No growth in dividends
2. Constant growth in dividends
3. Variable growth in dividends

When a company pays consistent dividends, which is usually the case with preferred stock, it is referred to as a perpetuity, which is a form of annuity. If you recall, this was one of the examples mentioned as a type of annuity in our time value of money section. This type of stock is called a *hybrid security*, because it has some features of a bond (annuity payments in the form of a consistent dividend that does not change), but unlike a bond, there is no maturity date, and while the dividend of a preferred stockholder must be paid prior to common stockholders receiving any dividends, there is no contractual obligation like bonds, and a company cannot default if they do not pay preferred stockholders.

In order to find the value of a preferred stock, we need to know the dividend and the required rate of return. If a preferred stock pays $4 and the required rate of return is 12%, what is the price of the stock? We can use the following formula:

Price of Preferred Stock = Dividend / Required Rate of Return

P = $4 / .12 = $33.33

You might be wondering why we do not use the time value of money annuity function in order to solve this. We can, but by definition, a perpetuity has *no end date*. Therefore, it would be difficult to find a number for N. But there is a workaround, we could simply use 100 years as N. While that number does not represent eternity, it is high enough to substitute in our problem. Go ahead and try it.

PMT = 4
I/Y = 12
N = 100
PV = -33.33

For common stock, we use a formula called the Gordon Growth Model, which is based on the idea that a company that issues dividends is going to issue them at a constant rate of growth. The formula is as follows:

$P_0 = D_1 / r - g$

Here, P_0 stands for the price of the stock today, hence the 0, which is the point in time we are referencing. D_1 stands for the dividend one time period later (in this case, one year, hence the number 1). The "r" stands for required rate of return, and "g" stands for the rate of growth the company expects to grow the dividend.

Using this model, we can find the value of a price of stock today. Suppose a company currently pays a dividend of $2, and has an expected growth rate of 5%. If the required rate of return of the company is 10%, then what is the current price of the stock?

Notice that the dividend of $2 is today's dividend, or D_0. In order to solve this, we need D_1. So our first step is to multiply $2 by the growth rate:

$2 x 1.05 = $2.10

(As a side note: Some students do not understand why we add a 1 in front of our converted percentage. The reason is the new dividend is going to be 100% + 5% of its current value, or 1.05 in decimal form.)

Now we can solve our problem:

$P_0 = \$2.10 / (.10 - .05) = \$2.10 / .05 = \$42.00$

Our final example of when a company is experiencing variable growth is going to combine the elements of time value of money we have already learned, as well as elements of the Gordon Growth Model.

Let's say a company is paying dividends of $3.00 in year one, $4.00 in year two, and $4.25 in year three, and expects to begin a constant growth rate of 4% from that point on. How do we value this kind of stock, that starts off with a high growth rate and eventually tapers and settles to 4% and the required rate of return is 10%? What is the total present value of the stock? We need to solve this type of problem in several steps.

First we need to find the present value of the dividends, which are all present value of a lump sum problem:

Year 1: FV = $3.00, N = 1, I/Y = 10, PV = ? = $2.73
Year 2: FV = $4.00, N = 2, I/Y = 10, PV = ? = $3.30
Year 3: FV = $4.25, N = 3, I/Y = 10, PV = ? = $3.19

Now we can determine the value of the stock in year three using the Gordon Growth Model, because it is in year four that the constant dividend growth rate begins. If you recall our formula $P_0 = D_1 / r - g$, it follows that $P_3 = D_4 / r - g$. First we need to find D_4 by multiplying D_3 by the growth rate.

$4.25 x 1.04 = $4.42

Then we divide this by (r - g) to get P_3. $4.42 / (.10 - .04) = $4.42 / .06 = $73.67. Since this number, P_3 is still not our present value, we need to perform yet another present value of a lump sum problem.

Price in year 3: FV = $73.67, N = 3, I/Y = 10, PV = ? = $55.35

Now that we have all the values for cash flows in year zero, we total them to get P_0:

$55.35 + $2.73 + $3.30 + $3.19 = $64.57

SECTION 7.7: DIVIDENDS

As can be seen, preferred and common stock dividends are critical components to valuation. They represent the future cash flows of a stock that are discounted back to the present to determine the value of the stock. As a point of review, it should be mentioned that cash dividends are paid out of the profits of the firm. There are other forms of dividends, however. Common stockholders can sometimes be paid in the form of stock dividends, where, instead of receiving cash, they receive extra shares or even fractional shares of stock. Some investors prefer stock dividends, as they are not taxed like cash dividends are.

Section 8.1: Capital Budgeting

Capital budgeting is the decision-making process a financial manager goes through when determining how to spend the money the company has available to them. There are any number of major expenditures a company could make, and understanding the potential cash flows that would result from those decisions, as well as how much it costs to generate capital, are both important.

As we discussed in the valuation section, the present value of any investment is based on its future cash flows discounted at an appropriate rate of return. When we apply this to the capital budgeting process, the cash flows are those that are expected from taking on a project or investment, and the rate of return we use has to exceed the cost of funds we borrowed or the rate of return expected by our shareholders.

Therefore, our capital budgeting analysis is only going to be as good as the inputs we use to do our calculations. While working capital management deals with the short-term assets and liabilities of a firm and how they are managed, capital budgeting involves planning for expenditures that last longer than one year (fixed assets and long-term expenditures such as in long-term securities), and how they are funded, usually through some combination of internally and externally generated funds such as retained earnings, stocks, bonds, preferred stocks, loans, and more.

As the planning time period gets longer, the results and assumptions become more uncertain. That is why regular monitoring and adjustments to capital budgeting plans need to be made. Just as with the daily review of working capital management, a regular plan for capital expenditures and the returns received from them is important to ensure projections are accurate and the company will remain solvent, and not become strained under excessive interest payments or high required rates of return.

SECTION 8.2: CAPITAL ASSETS

Capital assets for businesses are considered any investment in property, plant, and equipment, or even long-term securities that are not meant to be liquidated for cash in the near term, but held as investments or used in the course of operating the business.

For example, when a company is expanding, they may purchase land to build a new plant, and then purchase equipment to fill this building to run the business operations. These are all examples of capital assets. They are meant to be long-term investments, and in particular, they should be purchased with the intention to generate cash flows. This is an important point. Capital assets should only be purchased if they are necessary in running a business. A company must plan very carefully to ensure capital is spent wisely, or else their stockholders and bondholders will soon take notice that their expenditures are not providing an adequate return on investment.

SECTION 8.3: BUDGETING AND EQUIPMENT

What types of activities need to be considered in the capital budgeting process? As mentioned, any expenditures that will last for more than one year.

Decisions may be made to replace outdated equipment with new equipment that will increase production times and, therefore, cash flows. Brand new equipment to expand a product line or go into a completely different business area to gain new market share may be considered. Sometimes capital expenditures on equipment occur due to new regulations that a company must adhere to in terms of safety in the workplace or more strict environmental standards, or equipment needed for research and development. A company should always plan some buffer into their budgets for these types of unexpected or experimental expenditures.

Obviously, no company is going to have limitless funds to use for any purpose they want at any time. Sometimes there will be enough funding to spend on several projects. These projects are considered independent, and sometimes, multiple independent projects can be funded as long as there is capital available to do so. Companies will look to all the different areas of the firm to work together to come up with proposals for mutually exclusive projects. Maybe a car company is looking to determine which version of a new car is going to be the most profitable. This is going to require considerable planning, but they know they cannot make two versions of the same car for sale and just see which one customers will like best. They have to do research, plan, and make the best decision for which car version and features are going to be most profitable, and plan their expenditures accordingly to build that car and essentially, hope for the best!

When a company commits to one mutually exclusive project, by definition, they exclude all other possibilities, and once capital expenditures are made, it would be very difficult to unwind them. This is why the budgeting process is so important and often involves all areas of the company, not just finance and accounting. Marketing, engineering, research, and more groups are going to be involved in this decision-making process. Then, with all available information, it is the job of the financial manager to forecast the cash flows associated with the purchase of the assets and execution of the project to the ultimate sales that will result. In this way, capital budgeting is the process of defining the strategic vision of a company, because it locks a company in to a specific set of activities.

SECTION 8.4: PROJECT CASH FLOW FORECASTING AND ANALYSIS

It is worth mentioning again that as we learned in our section on the financial statements, there is a difference between profits and cash flows. Capital budgeting is only concerned with cash flows, and in order for the assumptions to be accurate, all future cash flows from a particular planned expenditure must be known.

To review, we add back depreciation after we determine our total earnings, in order to determine total cash flow for a period:

EBITDA	$10,000
Depreciation	$4,000
EBIT	$6,000
Interest	$1,000
Taxes (30%)	$1,500
EAT	$3,500
Depreciation	$4,000
Cash Flow	**$7,500**

When planning cash flows from a specific project, there are several ways you can look at determining them.

SECTION 8.5: INCREMENTAL CASH FLOWS

When a company evaluates cash flows, they will want to determine the incremental cash flow from operations they receive from a project over time. In this section, we will consider just the first year, in which there is an initial cost or outflow of funds to fund the project, and how that will change revenues and expenses (before taxes, for the sake of simplicity).

In order to determine incremental cash flows, the financial manager needs to know the initial outlay (the total upfront expenses of the project) and any cash inflows or outflows as a result of taking on the project. For now we are going to consider the first year of operations.

We can use this simple formula as a basis for understanding incremental cash flows:

Revenues – Expenses – Initial Outlay = Incremental Cash Flows

Keep in mind, the capital budgeting decision that is being made is not in a vacuum, but it is made against the alternative of doing whatever the current path is, versus the proposed path. Therefore, we further consider the incremental cash flows between two options (such as continuing the current path versus a new project, or between two mutually exclusive projects). For example, if a project is going to earn net cash flows of $100,000, and the current operations yields net cash flows of $75,000, there is only a net gain of $25,000, not $100,000. This is an important point to understand.

In this case, we would need to update our formula to include:

Change in Revenues (between two alternatives) – Change in Expenses – Initial Outlay = Incremental Cash Flow

Suppose a company has revenues of $250,000 and expenses of $75,000. They plan to purchase new machinery in the amount of $80,000. They expect revenues to increase to $350,000 and expenses to increase to $125,000. What will their incremental cash flow (before taxes and depreciation) be in the first year?

Change in revenues: $350,000 - $250,000 = $100,000 (increase)
Change in expenses: $125,000 - $75,000 = $50,000 (increase)
Initial outlay: $80,000

Incremental cash flow: $100,000 - $50,000 - $80,000 = -$30,000

We can see the first year has a negative cash flow. Does that mean we should not undertake this project? We actually do not have enough information to determine this yet. We would need to project our cash flows into the future, as well as determine the potential terminal value and cash flows when the project ends and we sell the machinery, if possible. We will take a more robust look at this in the next section where we discuss total project cash flows.

SECTION 8.6: TOTAL CASH FLOWS

In order to determine if a project will be profitable and is worth undertaking, the financial manager needs to determine the potential life of the project. For example, will this project, the machinery used to produce it, and these revenue figures continue for several years? Will we be able to sell any equipment at the start of the project (retiring old equipment) or sell the machinery at the end of the project? Can we depreciate the cost of the equipment over time, and what are the tax implications of the project? As you can see, there are many questions when it comes to determining the total cash flows of a project.

Additionally, there is the concept we have discussed throughout the text: the time value of money, and using that to determine how the discount rate affects discounting those future project cash flows back to the present, in order to determine the total present value of the project, which is also known as net present value, or NPV. There are a lot of moving parts, and it is important to know what they are and track them carefully.

One important item that affects total cash flows is depreciation. We have already discussed that depreciation is a non-cash expense, sometimes referred to as a phantom expense, because it never actually happens and never results in a cash outflow. This is important to understand, and the reason we add depreciation back for cash flows purposes. When new equipment is purchased, a business will get a depreciation allowance for the full cost—as well as any costs to begin using the equipment, such as installation, or in very rare cases, even the cost to train employees to use highly specialized equipment.

How does a company determine how much of an asset's value to allow for depreciation in any one year? There are two methods: straight line depreciation, where the value is divided over a number of years equally, or a modified accelerated cost recovery system, or MACRS schedule, which allows for greater depreciation expense deductions in the first few years of operating the new equipment, when the need for extra cash is usually the highest.

With straight line depreciation, an asset costing $100,000 with a ten-year life (the general amount of time the business believes the asset will fully operate), will have a $10,000 depreciation allowance each year: $100,000 x .10 = $10,000. Under a MACRS depreciation system, which is published by the IRS and may be subject to occasional changes, they will be allowed the following percentages over ten years: 10%, 18%, 14.4%, 11.5%, 9.2%, 7.4%, 6.6%, 6.5%, 6.5%, and 3.3%. If you were counting, you may have noticed there are eleven amounts here. This is because there is a half-year convention in the year the asset is sold.

Another expense that affects net cash flows from a project is corporate taxes. It is important to note that the corporate tax rate is often subject to change on an annual basis. As of the writing of this document, the corporate tax rate is 20%, but there are many types of taxes and fees that businesses must pay when looking at investing in a new project. Some businesses get large tax breaks if they work in an area that the government is particularly interested in supporting, such as environmental or medical research.

In the next section, we will look at how all cash flows over time affect the final decision to invest or not invest in a project.

SECTION 8.7: PRO FORMA CASH FLOW

Just as we created a cash budget in section 6.8, a pro forma cash flow (pro forma simply means *projection*) needs to be made for any project we undertake. Let's look at an example.

Suppose a company buys equipment that costs $200,000 and has a five-year life. We have crunched the numbers and believe this equipment will generate an additional $74,000 of earnings before interest, taxes, and depreciation (revenues minus expenses) for the first three years, then $48,000 for the last three years. (Remember, a four-year life still has a final half-year allowance.) We will assume a corporate tax rate of 20%. The MACRS five-year schedule is as follows: 20%, 32%, 19.2%, 11.5%, 11.5%, and 5.8%.

First, we just look at the pro forma cash flows associated with the operation of the new equipment:

	Year 1	Year 2	Year 3	Year 4	Year 5	Year 6
EBITDA	$74,000	$74,000	$74,000	$48,000	$48,000	$48,000
Depreciation	$40,000	$64,000	$38,400	$23,000	$23,000	$11,600
EBT	$34,000	$10,000	$35,600	$25,000	$25,000	$36,400
Taxes (20%)	$6,800	$2,000	$7,120	$5,000	$5,000	$7,280
EAT	$27,200	$8,000	$28,480	$20,000	$20,000	$29,120
+ Depreciation	$40,000	$64,000	$38,400	$23,000	$23,000	$11,600
Cash Flow	**$67,200**	**$72,000**	**$66,880**	**$43,000**	**$43,000**	**$40,720**

In the next sections we will discuss how we can further analyze this example.

SECTION 8.8: FINANCIAL ANALYSIS TOOLS

When a company faces a capital budgeting decision, they have many tools available to them. We will briefly look at five methods.

SECTION 8.9: NET PRESENT VALUE

The first method we will look at when deciding whether or not to accept a project is called the net present value, or NPV. This is where we take all the cash flows of a project and discount them back to the present time using an appropriate rate of return, usually the business' cost of capital. We will discuss how cost of capital is determined later, but for now just understand that it is the cost the business needs to pay to use the capital they raise.

Once we discount each cash flow to the present time, we compare that figure to the initial outlay, and if the number is positive, it means the project was profitable and we should accept taking on the project. If the number is negative, we should not accept the project, because it means we have lost money.

Let's use the cash flows from our above example and discount them back to the present (lump sum of a future value) using a cost of capital of 8%. (Round to the nearest dollar.)

Cash Flow Year 1: FV = $67,200, N = 1, I/Y = 8, PV = $62,222
Cash Flow Year 2: FV = $72,000, N = 2, I/Y = 8, PV = $61,728
Cash Flow Year 3: FV = $66,880, N = 3, I/Y = 8, PV = $53,092
Cash Flow Year 4: FV = $43,000, N = 4, I/Y = 8, PV = $31,606
Cash Flow Year 5: FV = $43,000, N = 5, I/Y = 8, PV = $29,265
Cash Flow Year 6: FV = $40,720, N = 6, I/Y = 8, PV = $25,661
Total Present Value of Cash Flows: $263,574

Now we subtract the initial outlay of $200,000, which does not need to be discounted as that cash flow already occurs in the present:

$263,574 - $200,000 = $63,574

The $63,574 represents the net present value of the project after the initial costs are taken into consideration. It is a positive value, therefore, by this criteria, the project should be undertaken.

For the sake of argument, let's say the cash flows totaled to only $180,000, what would the result be?

$180,000 - $200,000 = -$20,000

A negative net present value would mean the business loses money on the project and it should be rejected.

There is a second way that NPV can be found using the TI BA II Plus financial calculator that takes fewer steps. It requires learning new buttons on the calculator, so let's familiarize ourselves with them first.

The CF button stands for cash flows, and we use this button any time we are doing NPV or as you will see later, IRR problems. The other button you will need is the down arrow button in the top row, #. You should also know there is a specific way to clear the calculator after doing a problem that stores cash flows using the CF button.

To clear cash flows, press: 2ND CF CE|C

Remember, the financial calculator is a computer that stores values, so be sure that you clear the correct way for the different types of problems.

Now let's look at how we solve for NPV using the cash flows buttons.

Step 1: Press CF, $200,000, then the S button to make it negative since it is the initial outflow, and then we press CF, ENTER and # one time. You should now see a C01 on the screen.
Step 2: Now enter the second cash flow of $67,200, press ENTER, and # # twice.
Step 3: Repeat for each cash flow, pressing ENTER, and # # twice each time.
Step 4: After the last cash flow, press the NPV button, and you will see I =
Step 5: Press 8 (for 8% cost of capital), then press ENTER # and you will see NPV = 0.00, which is the prompt to press the CPT (compute) button. You should get $63,574 (rounded to the nearest dollar).

SECTION 8.10: PAYBACK

The payback method is considered a less sophisticated way to determine the acceptability of a project, yet many businesses use it nonetheless for its simplicity. It does not take into consideration a rate of return. The only criteria is *how quickly* the original investment cost is recovered.

Consider two projects with the following cash flows and an initial outlay of $8,000:

	Project A	Project B
Cash Flow 1	$1,000	$5,000
Cash Flow 2	$2,000	$3,000
Cash Flow 3	$3,000	$1,000
Cash Flow 4	$8,000	$1,000

As we can see, if we are considering the payback method, we would be more likely to accept Project B, because at some point in the second year, we have earned all our initial costs back. However, there are major drawbacks to this method. As mentioned, there is no discount rate used in this method, and it ignores both cash flows that come later and total cash flows. Project A has a considerable cash flow in year four, as well as total higher flows, but it still might be rejected under the payback method because for some businesses who are less credit worthy and simply need their cash back as fast as possible, Project B is still the better choice.

Going back to our original example, in what year would the company make back their money under the payback method? We simply subtract each cash flow from the initial outlay until we know which year they make their money back:

	Cash flows	Remaining Balance
Year 0	($200,000)	($200,000)
Year 1	$67,200	($132,800)
Year 2	$72,000	($60,800)
Year 3	$66,880	$6,080

As we can see, at some point in year three, the money is paid back.

SECTION 8.11: ACCOUNTING RATE OF RETURN

The accounting rate of return is another way to determine if a project is acceptable using capital budgeting rules. Similar to the payback method, it is a simple way to calculate a return on investment, and the time value of money and timing of cash flows is not considered.

The formula used is:

Accounting Rate of Return: Average Annual Accounting Profit / Initial Outlay

Notice that the numerator is profits, *not* cash flows. This is an important distinction, and going back to our example, we would need to use the EAT figure, not the cash flow figure.

First we add the annual profits (EAT) and divide by the number of years to get the average annual accounting profit:

Total EAT: $27,200 + $8,000 + $28,480 + $20,000 + $20,000 + $29,120 = $132,800
Average EAT: $132,800 / 6 = $22,133

Accounting rate of return: $22,133 / $200,000 = 11.07\%$

If you recall, earlier we stated the company's cost of capital was 8%. This means that the accounting rate of return is greater than the costs, so using this method, we would accept the project.

SECTION 8.12: INTERNAL RATE OF RETURN

The internal rate of return, or IRR, is a method of calculating the return on any single investment. In the example we have been looking at, that would be this one particular project, as opposed to the returns in the business as a whole.

The reason we would want to know the rate of return or yield from one project is so we can assess it against other options, as well as against the company's cost to finance the project. Just as net present value compared the dollar value of cash flows against the initial outlay using the company's cost of capital, the IRR also utilizes the same information, but instead of setting a discount rate (a rate of return), this method calculates the rate of return that equates the cash outflows with their subsequent inflows, and compares *that* number to the cost of capital.

If the internal rate of return is higher than the cost of capital, it would be a project worth undertaking, because it would mean that the project is earning more money than the rate it takes to fund it. However, if the IRR is lower than the cost of capital, then the project is losing money and should not be undertaken.

Since we already learned to use the cash flows buttons on the NPV problem above, just know we will follow the exact same series of steps, with the exception of pressing NPV at the end. This is because we are not looking for NPV, of course, but for IRR.

Instead, we will press the IRR button and CPT and get our percentage rate of return answer. Let's try it with our above example.

First clear the calculator by pressing:
CF 2ND CE|C

Then enter CF $200,000 S ENTER #
$67,200 ENTER ##
$72,000 ENTER ##
$66,880 ENTER ##
$43,000 ENTER ##
$43,000 ENTER ##
$40,720 ENTER ##

Then press IRR and CPT and you get 19.18%, which is far more than the 8% cost of the project, so we would accept the project. As you can see, this is a much higher rate than the cost of capital, and we should consider the reasons why this might be. The IRR method assumes each cash flow can be reinvested at the same rate of return as the overall investment, which may not be true. While the project might yield 19.18%, we may not be able to invest every subsequent cash flow at the same rate. This is one of the main drawbacks of the IRR method as a capital budgeting criteria.

SECTION 8.13: BREAK-EVEN AND SENSITIVITY ANALYSIS

A company will always want to know their break-even point. That is the point at which their revenues equal their expenses. By definition, this means zero profit has been made.

The formula for the break-even point would be:

Break-even = Fixed Costs / (Sales price per unit – Variable cost per unit)

The fixed costs for a project would be all initial cost or outlays, the sales price would be at what price we sell the product we produce, and the variable costs are all costs per unit incurred in the course of production of the goods for sale.

Let's say the fixed costs in our example are $200,000, and the sales price is $500 with variable costs per unit of $100. What is our break-even?

Break-even = $200,000 / ($500 - $100) = $200,000 / $400 = 500 units

We would need to sell 500 units to break even.

The final, but very important method of capital budgeting that bears mentioning is sensitivity analysis. While the full scope of sensitivity analysis techniques is beyond the scope of this text, the concept is not and can be understood intuitively. That is, that all the assumptions we input into any capital budgeting method yields results that are only as good as those inputs. Therefore, it is a good business practice to change and challenge our assumptions and test them against different scenarios and see how the numbers may change. The goal with sensitivity analysis is to assess risk and how much variability we are willing to handle in our assumptions.

In broad terms, sensitivity analysis works by changing one variable in a project at a time, so that it can be tested while keeping other variables constant, and then seeing how the outcome of the project changes. To use our above example of the break-even analysis: perhaps we want to change our variable cost and make it higher to account for the increase in the price of raw materials projected in the coming year. If we increase our variable costs to $150, how does that change our break-even?

$200,000 / ($500 - $150) = $200,000 / $350 = 572$ units (we round up because we cannot make .43 units of a good)

As we can see, we now need to plan to sell 72 more units than before to break even. We would then need to determine if we think that we can do so.

 # Section 9.1: Cost of Capital

Cost of capital has been mentioned above as the cost of financing the company's capital. When a company needs funding to start their company or new growth opportunities, they have to find sources of capital. This can come in the form of internally generated funds from profits, or externally generated funds such as borrowing from a lender, issuing bonds of differing times to maturity to bondholders, or issuing stock to common or preferred stockholders.

Each of these sources of funds has a cost associated with it. For example, a bondholder expects a certain rate of return (which is what they earn on their investment), and the same rate of return is a *cost* to the company. Generally, a company will seek several different types of funding in order to diversify their sources of capital, and thereby can reduce their overall costs as well as risk. This is because certain forms of funding are riskier than others. Generally speaking, bond funding is considered a bit riskier, especially if it funds more than 50% of the capital of a company. The reason is that bonds require interest payments to bondholders, which is a contractual obligation that must be paid or the company is considered to be in default. Therefore, the ability to diversify sources of capital to reduce risk and costs is very important.

We will see later how we can calculate the overall cost of capital by weighting each source of capital to determine total overall costs, which is the cost of capital to the company for their operations and any project they undertake.

SECTION 9.2: COST OF DEBT

As mentioned, each source of capital has its own cost associated with it. The cost of debt is the yield to maturity, or YTM, which is the theoretical rate of return a bondholder will earn if they hold the bond to maturity. In turn, this same rate of return represents an interest payment that must be paid by the company and is a component in the cost of debt. The reason the YTM and cost of debt are not equal is because a company gets a tax deduction for interest payments. In an earlier section we learned how to determine the present value of a bond. Now we are going to use time value of money calculations in order to determine the YTM of a bond. Then, once we find the YTM, we have to deduct the tax rate to determine the after-tax cost of debt, which will be lower due to the tax deduction benefit.

A company may have several types of loans and debt they utilize, which will all determine their cost of debt. The more debt a company holds, the more leveraged they are and the riskier they are, therefore, the higher their cost of debt will generally be. Whether a company is a large company issuing bonds in the market, or if it is a small business that secures a loan from a bank or even relatives, it is the same concept—the interest they owe is their cost of capital.

Suppose a company has a bond outstanding with ten years to maturity, with a face value of $1,000, a coupon of 7%, and is currently selling for $950 in the open market. What is the YTM associated with this bond?

First, we need to set up our variables. Remember that when we are doing bond valuation time value of money problems we need to pay close attention to the cash flows. If we look at these problems from the point of view of the bondholder, we know the face value/future value and coupon payments will be an inflow to us, and the present value is a cost to us today, or an outflow.

$1,000 = FV
10 = N
$70 = PMT
-$950 = PV
Press I/Y, then CPT = 7.74%

As we can see, the YTM is slightly higher than the coupon of 7%, because the bond is selling at a discount. However, our cost calculation is not complete, because we need to determine the tax effect. We use the following formula:

Cost of debt x (1 – Tax rate) = After-tax cost of debt capital

In our above example, let's say the tax rate is 30%.

7.74% x (1 - .30) = 7.74% x .70 = 5.42% is the after-tax cost of capital for this debt

SECTION 9.3: COST OF EQUITY

When a company seeks equity financing, they are issuing shares in the company, which represents an ownership stake. As partial owners of the company, stockholders are entitled to a portion of the profits in the form of dividends, and also expect the stock price to increase over time, which determines the overall rate of return of the stock.

Again, the rate of return the stockholders expect is the cost to the company to use that particular source of financing.

If you have heard of an initial public offering, or an IPO, that is when a company first goes out into the open market and sells their shares for the first time. As discussed above, if you are a small business owner who raises funds from friends and family who expect to participate in the returns you receive, you should realize you are actually issuing equity and they have become partial owners. Those owners are taking a chance on the business, large or small, and expect to be compensated for the risk of using their funds in the business. We will now look at how those costs are calculated.

SECTION 9.4: COMMON AND PREFERRED STOCK

Earlier, we looked at common and preferred stock valuation, which involved determining the price of a share of stock. We can use the same formulas: the Gordon Growth Model formula and perpetuity valuation formula, and rearrange them algebraically in order to isolate the rate of return variable in each: r.

Let's begin by recalling the original Gordon Growth Model formula:

$$P0 = D1 / (r-g)$$

If we rearrange it to isolate r, we get:

$$r = (D1 / P0) +g$$

If a company is planning to issue a dividend of $2.50 next year, and has a current price of $25.00 and expects a growth rate of 3%, what is their rate of return?

$$r = \$2.50/\$25.00 + .03 = .10 + .03 = .13 \text{ or } 13\%$$

There is no tax deduction for equity, so the required rate of return will simply equal the cost of equity to the company.

The formula used for the value of a perpetuity (preferred stock) is:

$$P = D/r$$

Rearranging it, we get:

$$r = D/P$$

If a preferred stock is priced at $11 and pays a dividend of $2, what is the yield?

$r = \$2/\$11 = 18.18\%$

SECTION 9.5: WEIGHTED AVERAGE COST OF CAPITAL

Now that we have determined how to calculate the costs of individual sources of capital, we can look at how we determine the overall cost of capital for the entire company, based on these sources, their individual costs, and their weights.

Weighting simply means how much of the total funding is comprised of a particular source of capital.

For example, if a company is funded by $100 million in debt and $100 million in equity, that would mean the company is weighted 50/50 debt to equity. If a company has $100 million in debt, $100 million in equity, and $100 million in preferred equity, it is easy to see the weights would be split into equal thirds, or 33.33333%. We will look at additional examples.

Suppose a company has $56 million in debt, $24 million in equity, and $18 million in preferred stock, how can we go about determining the weights of each?

First we must add up all three sources of funding to determine the total amount of capital:

$56 + $24 + $18 = $98 million

Now each weight is determined by dividing its share into $98 million, or the total.

Weight of debt = $56/$98 = 57.14%
Weight of equity = $24/$98 = 24.49%
Weight of preferred stock = $18/$98 = 18.37%

The reason we want to know the weights of each source of capital is that if we then multiply the weight of each source by the cost of each source of capital, we can then determine the costs of each portion of capital, then add it up to get the total cost of capital. This idea is summarized in the weighted average cost of capital, or WACC, formula. The WACC is the discount rate that must be applied to any project a company undertakes, regardless of the source of capital used to fund it. This is because all capital is pooled and the costs must be shared across all operations. In this way, the WACC is also known as a "hurdle rate" that all projects must meet to break even or exceed to be profitable.

WACC = (Weight of debt x After-tax cost of debt) + (Weight of equity x Cost of equity) + (Weight of preferred stock x Cost of preferred stock)

Let's look at a simple example, where the weights and costs are given. If a company has 40% debt, 30% equity, and 30% preferred equity, and the cost of debt (after-tax) is 5.6%, the cost of equity is 7.2%, and the cost of preferred stock is 6.0%, what is the overall cost of capital?

WACC = (.40 x .056) + (.30 x .072) + (.30 x .06)
      = (.0224) + (.0216) + (.018)
      = .062 or 6.2%

Now let's look at a more comprehensive example, where we need to determine all aspects of the weighted average cost of capital, as well as the costs for each source of capital. In doing so, we will see how the WACC calculation builds upon what we have learned about time value of money, as well as debt, equity, and preferred stock valuation.

Suppose a company has debt in the amount of $120 million, equity of $85 million, and preferred stock of $25 million. The bonds outstanding have a face value of $1,000, fifteen years left to maturity, a coupon of 8%, and are being sold in the market for $970. The common stock is selling at a price of $42.50, with the most recent dividend paid of $2.75, and a projected growth rate of 5% in the future. The preferred stock price is $52 and the dividend is $3.50, indefinitely. With a tax rate of 30%, what is this company's weight average cost of capital?

First we need to determine the weights of each source of capital.

Total capital = $120 + $85 + $25 = $230 in total capital

Weight of debt = $120/$230 = 52.17%
Weight of equity = $85/$230 = 36.96%
Weight of preferred equity = $25/$230 = 10.9%

Now we need to determine the cost of each source of capital. Let's begin with the debt component.

$1,000 = FV
15 = N
$80 = PMT
-$970 = PV
I/Y = ? = 8.4%

Remember, the YTM is not the final cost of debt. We need to multiply the YMT by 1-tax rate to determine the after-tax cost of debt, which is the cost to the company.

8.4% x (1 - .30) = 8.4% x .70 = 5.88% = after-tax cost of debt

Next we determine the rate of return on common equity using the rearranged Gordon Growth Model:

r = (D1/ P0) + g

D0 = $2.75
D1 = $2.75 x 1.05 = $2.89

r = ($2.89/$42.50) + .05
r = .068 + .05 = .1180 or 11.80%

Finally we determine the cost of preferred stock using the rate of return of a perpetuity formula:

r = D/P

r = $3.50 / $52 = .067 or 6.7%

Now that we have found every variable that goes into our equation, we can solve for WACC:

WACC = (.5217 x .0588) + (.3696 x .1180) + (.109 x .067)
       = (.0307) + (.0436) + (.0073)
       = .0816 or 8.16%

While the process of solving a WACC problem can seem lengthy, simply approaching each variable in a methodical way, solving each section one part at a time until you have listed all the variables (individual weights and costs), then combining them into the final WACC calculation is straightforward.

Section 10.1: Risk and Return

Risk is the concept of quantifying uncertainty, or the variability of outcomes in a possible situation. There is what is known as the risk and return tradeoff, which is the idea that the greater the risk one undertakes, the greater the potential upside, but also the greater potential downside losses. Conversely, the less risk one undertakes, the less potential gains or losses one will subject themselves to. When considering risk in the context of corporate finance, there are tools we can use to measure and assess risk.

SECTION 10.2: EXPECTED RETURN ON AN ASSET AND A PORTFOLIO

Throughout this text we have made reference to rates of return, and so far, most of these rates were given variables or they were determined by knowing many other variables about a particular investment, project, or source of capital. YTM, r, and IRR are all examples of expected rates of return. Returns can be measured for any individual security or a portfolio of securities, which is a collection of investments of different amounts. A portfolio can take almost any form or combination of stocks, bonds, and other types of investments. When we look at any investment, whether alone or in a portfolio, it is beneficial to have a way to measure the expected return and risk of the investment.

SECTION 10.3: MEASURES OF RISK

There are two main measures of risk we will consider: beta and standard deviation.

Beta is one of the most well-known risk measures, and it measures the volatility of returns on an individual stock, relative to the stock market as a whole. What this means is that any individual stock is going to have some relationship to the stock market as a whole. If the stock market rises, some stocks will rise, some will fall, and some may stay even. The amount of variability any one stock experiences in relation to the market is how volatile (sensitive to changes) it is. Beta measures that volatility. By definition, a stock with a beta of one will track exactly the same as the market. For example, if the stock market, as measured by the Dow Jones Industrial Average, rises by 5%, then so will this stock. It is important to remember, these are theoretical measures and not predictive ones. The actual performance of a stock is going to be based on many factors, but when evaluating stocks for investing, you have to have some basis for why you are investing, and beta is one of the tools you can use.

It follows then, that a beta that is greater than one will mean that individual stock is *more* volatile than the market as a whole, and a beta less than one will be less volatile than the market as a whole.

Standard deviation is another widely used method to assess the risk of a stock or a portfolio. The technical definition is that standard deviation is a measure of the dispersion, or variance, of a set of data from its mean. Dispersion or variance is another way of saying how far away something is from something else, a set of data is just going to be a set of numbers, and a mean is the average of that same set of numbers.

Standard deviation is calculated by first taking a set of data points and finding their mean. In order to do that the number of data points is counted and given the variable name n (number of data points). Next, the mean is subtracted from each data point, and squared. Those values are added up and then divided by n-1, and the square root of that figure is the standard deviation.

This process is most easily understood through an example.

Suppose we have the following data points:

Data Points
2
5
7
4
2

Our n = 5 because there are five data points. Our mean is going to be the sum of the data points divided by n.

Mean = 2 + 5 + 7 + 4 + 2 = 20/5 = 4

Now we need to subtract the mean from each data point to determine the variance:

Data Points	Mean	Variance
2	4	-2
5	4	1
7	4	3
4	4	0
2	4	-2

Next we need to square each variance and total them:

Data Points	Mean	Variance	Variance Squared
2	4	-2	4
5	4	1	1
7	4	3	9
4	4	0	0
2	4	-2	4
		Total	**18**

We then take the square root of 18 to determine the standard deviation, which is 4.2426.

SECTION 10.4: DETERMINANTS OF INTEREST RATES

When we consider the factors that go into determining interest rates for any particular investment, there are five components to consider. They are: the risk-free rate, inflation, the default risk premium, the liquidity premium, and the maturity premium. Not every component is a factor in every interest rate, but generally speaking, the risk-free rate, plus inflation, plus other risk factors, are involved in every type of investment.

In section 7.1, we discussed that the risk-free rate is only theoretically risk-free, and only as reliable as the sovereign government backing the securities, but it is the basis of returns that we should expect from all investments as a baseline. From there, the other components of interest rates are added based on economic factors and the risk inherent in a particular investment.

In section 4.1, we briefly discussed the fact that inflation causes an erosion in buying power over time, and most investors expect to be compensated for this risk when someone else is using their money.

The three risk premiums mentioned are based on various factors specific to any one investment. Default risk premium is the additional compensation an investor expects for taking on the risk that a company would be unable to make obligated payments on time or in full. Liquidity risk premium is the additional compensation an investor expects for the risk their money may be tied up in an investment that is not easily turned back into cash. The maturity risk premium is just that the longer an investment's time horizon is, the more uncertain the outcome will be, so additional compensation is required to make up for that uncertainty.

Risk premiums are assessed for the general creditworthiness and potential of a company. For example, a small cap stock (a smaller company that may be in its first few years of operations) will carry a higher risk premium because its business model is less established than a large cap company such as the well-known Coca-Cola or Disney, who have extremely long track records and loyal customers, who can enjoy a much smaller risk premium because investors feel their money is more safe there.

How can a total interest rate be determined using these components? Just by adding them up. For example, if the risk-free rate is 2%, inflation is 2%, and a small cap stock has a risk premium of 10%, what is the expected rate of return? It will be 2% + 2% + 10% = 14%, which is the interest rate investors will expect to earn for the risks they are taking on by giving their money to this investment.

SECTION 10.5: REAL AND NOMINAL INTEREST RATES

The difference between real and nominal interest rates is that nominal rates are the rates as stated, or *in name*, which is what nominal means. So, a 5% interest on a loan of $100 is going to be $5. However, the real interest rate differs from nominal in that it takes the effects of inflation into account to determine the real cost or buying power associated with the interest rate. In our same example, if inflation is 2%, then $2 of our $5 is essentially lost to the lender, because inflation is eroding that much of the value of the interest received over time.

SECTION 10.6: CAPITAL ASSET PRICING MODEL

The capital asset pricing model, or CAPM, is a way to determine the expected return on a stock using beta and other inputs into interest rates—just as we calculated *r* above for common equity and preferred stock using dividends and stock prices (a discounted cash flow model such as in sections 7 and 8). Specifically, the formula for CAPM is:

$$E_r = R_{fr} + B(R_m - R_{fr})$$

Where:

E_r = Expected Return
R_{fr} = Risk-free rate
B = Beta
R_m = Return on the market (as measured by some benchmark or proxy such as the Dow Jones Industrial Average)

If we assume the following values:

$R_{fr} = 2\%$
$B = 1.2$
$R_m = 8\%$

We can solve for the expected return using CAPM:

$E_r = .02 + 1.2(.08-.02) = .02 + 1.2(.06) = .02 + .72 = 7.4\%$

SECTION 10.7: SECURITY MARKET LINE

If one were to graph the capital asset pricing model on a chart with required rates of return on the Y-axis and beta on the X-axis, the line drawn is known as the security market line, or SML. In other words, for every given beta, an expected rate of return for the market as a whole is plotted. The usefulness of the SML is to determine if an investor is taking on too much risk, or earning too little of a rate of return based on its relationship to the line. For example, if a security is plotted above the line, it is an indication that it is being undervalued, since for a given beta (level of risk), it is earning a greater rate of return than the market as a whole. If a stock is plotted below the line, that means the investor is taking on more risk for less return, and other investment opportunities are available at a lower beta, which could return the same interest rate.

The slope of the SML is known as the market risk premium, which is the difference between the expected return on the market and the risk-free rate, just as we saw in the CAPM formula.

SECTION 10.8: DIVERSIFICATION

The risk in a portfolio of stocks is based on the risks of each investment and the weights they hold in your entire portfolio. It is important that you choose your investments wisely and diversify them—choose several or many different kinds of investments to reduce your total risk.

Diversification is a concept in modern portfolio theory, which you may know by the old folk wisdom, "Don't put all your eggs in one basket." The reason is, if that one basket spills, all your eggs could break. The same advice is applicable to investments. If you place all your money into one investment, you are committing to the risk and returns of that stock. Diversification is an important principle and a way to protect your capital by spreading risk among many investments

We should know there are two kinds of risk: systematic, or market risk, and company specific, or unsystematic risk.

Market risk cannot be diversified away, and it is the risk any investor takes in simply participating in the market. There are factors that sway the markets as a whole, but there can be hedges against certain market movements if you can anticipate them. However, that is different than diversification, as we will learn shortly.

Unsystematic risk is that which you can diversify away by investing in a variety of investments. More specifically, non-correlated investments that are in different industries and have opposite movements in the stock market. In theory, specific risk, that which is associated with a single investment or company, can be diversified away completely by choosing a perfectly negatively-correlated investment. To use an example, a tech stock might by perfectly negatively-correlated with a utility company, or at the very least, be different enough that neither stock is going to react exactly the same to different news or economic events.

Section 11.1: International Financial Management

As the world economy becomes more integrated, goods, funds, and information are exchanged at a much more rapid pace and at higher volumes. An event in one country can send shock waves through the entire global economy, as was seen during the 2008 economic crisis that had its inception in the United States real estate market and the default of trillions of dollars of subprime securities. But crises are not the only reason to pay attention to international markets. Anyone in business today needs to keep themselves knowledgeable about international financial issues.

Many businesses are multi-nationals and, as a result, it is impossible to avoid issues of politics, public health, equality, and more that occur in nations around the world, as they affect the employees, customers, and operations of firms worldwide. Free trade agreements are utilized to effect change and negotiate favorable trade terms between cooperating nations. The dissolution of such trade agreements can be damaging to one or both parties. Similarly, trade embargoes or tariffs can discourage trade and encourage competition instead of cooperation.

Currently, the U.S. dollar is considered the most stable international store of value, but during the 2008 crisis, the euro was briefly considered more stable. These events are always changing and there is often no telling when some kind of international issue will affect a business.

SECTION 11.2: IMPACT OF EXCHANGE RATES ON INTERNATIONAL FINANCIAL MARKETS

The simplest way to illustrate the effect of exchange rates on international financial markets is to imagine you are planning a trip abroad, perhaps to China. As of the writing of this text, one U.S. dollar will buy you 6.36 Chinese renminbi (the official currency in China). The buying power of 6.36 renminbi is also greater than what you could purchase in the U.S. for $1, so the buying power of a dollar goes much further in China. This relationship between the two currencies is known as the exchange rate.

The exchange rate relationship is constantly changing, and fluctuates on a daily basis, which is due to the *floating exchange system*, which is one where prices are determined by supply and demand for the currency, and is adopted by most nations. In contrast, a fixed exchange system is where the government of a country determines the price of a currency. There are also hybrids of the two systems, such as that used by China, where the renminbi is allowed to fluctuate, but only within a set range, and is tied to the U.S. dollar.

Financial managers need to be aware of and sensitive to these exchange rates if they transact business with other countries. Whether it is related to the purchase of raw materials, they may find their capital goes further in one country than it does in another. If they are trading their goods and services to other countries, they may want to know where they can benefit from exchange rates if customers purchase in one currency, which is then exchanged to U.S. dollars.

There are many factors that affect exchange rates, such as inflation, which result in considerable differences in buying power. Consider the British pound, which, as of this writing, one U.S. dollar is worth 0.72 British pounds, and yet that same 0.72 pounds buys much less than what a dollar can buy. This would make a trip to London very expensive for someone who earns money in U.S. dollars.

Interest rates can also influence exchange rates. As we discussed previously, investors are seeking to minimize risk, and maximize returns. If there are newly discovered opportunities in one country, it could increase the demand for trading in their currency, causing demand to rise, as well as the price to rise, making it more valuable in comparison to other currencies.

SECTION 11.3: CURRENCY RISK AND POLITICAL RISK

From our previous discussions of risk, it should be obvious that risk is a measure of potential loss and gain. Currency risk is another example where investors can gain or lose money from international transactions.

To use an example, let's imagine a U.S. investor has purchased a bond from a European company who pays in euros. That would mean a 1,000 euro bond with a 5% coupon rate pays 50 euro in interest. For the sake of argument, let's say the U.S. dollar and the euro are equal at the time of purchase with a $1 = 1 euro exchange rate. At this point in time, there would be no difference in holding a European bond and getting the 5% payment in euros to the U.S. investor, because $50 = 50 euro. However, if after five years' time has passed, the exchange rate is now $1 = .75 euro, then even though the investor is still receiving 50 euro in interest, it is no longer worth $50, but instead $37.50, so the exchange rate is very unfavorable, and the buying power of 50 euro has decreased considerably. This is the potential loss investors face with currency risk.

Holders of foreign bonds face currency risk, as those types of bonds make interest and principal payments in a foreign currency. For example, let's assume XYZ Company is a Canadian company and pays interest and principal on a $1,000 bond with a 5% coupon in Canadian dollars. If the exchange rate at the time of purchase is 1:1, then the 5% coupon payment is equal to $50 Canadian, and because of the exchange rate, it is also equal to U.S. $50. Now let's assume a year from now that the exchange rate is 1:0.85. Now the bond's 5% coupon payment, which is still $50 Canadian, is worth only U.S. $42.50. Despite the issuer's ability to pay, the investor has lost a portion of his return because of the fluctuation of the exchange rate.

Another major risk in international finance is political risk. It should come as no surprise that politics within a nation or between nations can have a major impact on business, on central banks, interest rates, the flow of funds, trade, and more. Every decision a country makes will affect their entire economy, and because all economies are connected, ripples can be felt throughout the world.

Business or investors who invest in developing nations take on extra risk because of political instability. For example, in some countries, private funds and businesses have been seized and nationalized without warning. This could devastate a business that has set up operations in such a country, and could result in the total loss of capital for their investors. While situations like this are rare, and potentially avoidable if one is careful about where they transact business, it does happen. Additionally, there is a sense of responsibility and agreement among nations, and even the mission of some companies, to invest in all countries, not only those that are the most stable, with the hopes that economic growth will lead to political freedom. Taking such a stand carries inherent political risk.

SECTION 11.4: TOOLS

There are tools to manage the risks in international finance. Due to the floating exchange rates, free markets, and freeing the flow of funds and international trade, currency fluctuations are more prominent than ever before. This has led to specific tools that are used in the management of foreign exchange risk.

SECTION 11.5: SPOT VS. FORWARD

There are two rates that are associated with every currency: the spot rate and the forward rate. The spot rate is the exchange rate a trader can get for immediate settlement on a currency. For example, if you went to your local currency exchange (often located in international airports, or possibly even your local bank in limited amounts) and you wish to buy Australian dollars, the banker will quote you the rate at which Australian dollars are currently selling, AUD 0.78/$. If you hand the banker $100, you will receive $78 AUD.

However, the forward market is when you are quoted a price to buy or sell a currency in the future. So, for example, let's say you are hoping to receive $78 AUD thirty days from now. However, there is no guarantee they will still cost you $100 by that point in time. You could purchase a forward contract to lock in your rate (which is based on market expectations, not what you wish to pay).

Because the forward rate deals with the future, the price you might be expected to pay in thirty, sixty, or ninety days will reflect what the market, in general, believes is going to happen to the value of the AUD in that time frame. As such, forward rates could be higher than spot rates (selling at a premium) or lower than spot rates (selling at a discount) to reflect that in the future.

Rates	AUD/USD
Spot	0.78
30 day forward	0.79
60 day forward	0.80

As can be seen in the above table, the thirty and sixty-day forward rate is trading at a premium (higher) compared to the spot rate. This means the market thinks the AUD value is going to increase in value relative to the U.S. dollar in the future.

SECTION 11.6: HEDGING

Because companies and investors are subject to foreign exchange risk, there is a strategy known as hedging, which helps to minimize those risks. Hedging allows an investor to protect their current position from unwanted rises or falls in exchange rates by locking in future rates.

One type of hedge most people already know about and use is insurance. For a premium (which is a fraction of the price of the protection you are purchasing), you are able to protect yourself or your valuable items from losses. While a hedge is not exactly the same as an insurance contract, it can similarly protect investments or the transaction of a business from losses that can occur due to currency fluctuations.

There are three main types of hedges related to foreign exchange risk: currency forwards, currency futures, and currency options.

Currency forwards can lock in the price of a currency at a future point in time, generally thirty, sixty, or ninety days. If you are a business who needs to deliver payment to a foreign company in ninety days, and exchange rates are favorable today, but you are not sure what they are going to do in the future, you could purchase a currency forward contract to lock in the price you want to pay in ninety days and then you can be certain of the price you will need to pay.

Currency futures are similar to forwards in that you can lock in a price of a currency at a future point in time, but they differ in that they are traded on a daily basis, and you could buy and sell them before the obligation date arrives. You may want to do this if rates change even more favorably, for example.

Currency options are contracts that can be bought or sold and give the right or obligation to buy or sell currencies at a specific price. Options are a broad and complicated topic and cannot be covered in depth in this text. However, the important features are that for a small premium price (the price of the option contract itself), you can lock in the right (but not the obligation) to purchase a currency at a pre-determined price and amount depending on the number of contracts you purchase.

 # Sample Test Questions

1) All of the following represent financial statements of the firm, except _____.

   A) The income statement
   B) The statement of liabilities
   C) The statement of cash flows
   D) The balance sheet

The correct answer is B:) The statement of liabilities. There is no statement by the name of statement of liabilities. Liabilities are contained within the balance sheet. (Section 1.2)

2) Current assets are also known as _____.

   A) Fixed assets
   B) Solid assets
   C) Intangible assets
   D) Liquid assets

The correct answer is D:) Liquid assets. Current assets are known as liquid assets because of their ability to be turned into cash in a short time period without losing much of their market value. (Section 1.2)

3) Property, plant, and equipment are also known as _____.

   A) Fixed assets
   B) Current assets
   C) Intangible assets
   D) Liquid assets

The correct answer is A:) Fixed assets. Property, plant, and equipment are considered fixed assets because they are meant to be utilized for a long period of time in the operations of the business. They also are not always able to be sold quickly or at a predictable value. (Section 1.2)

4) If the par value of a stock is $10 per share, and 10,000 shares were sold for a total value of $120,000, what is the capital in excess of par?

   A) $0
   B) $10,000
   C) $20,000
   D) $100,000

The correct answer is C:) $20,000. If par value is $10, then $10 x 10,000 equals $100,000. Total shares were sold for $120,000. Therefore, $120,000 - $100,000 = $20,000 is the capital in excess of par amount. (Section 1.2)

5) If Trisha's Trumpets, Inc. has $132 million in total assets, $87 million in total debt, what is the amount of owner's equity?

   A) $219 million
   B) $87 million
   C) $45 million
   D) $24 million

The correct answer is C:) $45 million. Total assets = Total liabilities + Owner's equity.
$132 million = $87 million + OE
$132 million - $87 million = OE
OE = $45 million
(Section 1.2)

6) The income statement is a measure of the _____ of a company.

   A) Debt utilization
   B) Profitability
   C) Marketability
   D) Asset turnover

The correct answer is B:) Profitability. The income statement begins with revenues, deducts a variety of expenses, and various profitability measures can then be determined, with net income and net profit being the final item. (Section 1.3)

7) Operating income is determined by the following equation:

    A) Revenues minus cost of goods sold
    B) Gross profit minus (SG&A and depreciation expense)
    C) EBIT minus interest expense
    D) Gross profit minus EBIT

The correct answer is B:) Gross profit minus (SG&A and depreciation expense). SG&A and depreciation are considered operating expenses. Therefore, deducting them from gross profit leaves you with the operating income, or the income remaining after operating expenses have been taken into consideration. (Section 1.3)

8) Cash flow from investing activities does not include:

    A) Sale of common stock of an outside company
    B) Purchase of common stock of an outside company
    C) Purchase of company's own common stock
    D) Sales of company's property

The correct answer is C:) Purchase of company's own common stock. This would be considered a cash flow from financing activities, as this relates to the company's own source of capital. (Section 1.4)

9) Increases in current assets are _____ on the statement of cash flows:

    A) Added to cash flows from operations
    B) Subtracted from cash flows from operations
    C) Added to cash flows from financing activities
    D) Subtracted from cash flows from financing activities

The correct answer is B:) Subtracted from cash flows from operations. Current assets are considering an operating account and part of cash flows from operating activities. An increase in current assets is a use of cash, therefore you must subtract it from cash flows from operations. (Section 1.4)

10) The statement of owner's equity includes net profits or losses, as well as
_____.

    A) Equity investments in other firms
    B) Owner's contributions of capital
    C) Bondholder claims on assets
    D) Total capital expenditures

The correct answer is B:) Owner's contributions of capital. The statement of owner's equity determines not only net income or loss from business operations, but also paid in capital or draws by the owners. (Section 1.5)

11) The quick ratio is a more _____ measure of a company's liquidity.

    A) Risky
    B) Unrealistic
    C) Speculative
    D) Conservative

The correct answer is D:) Conservative. The quick ratio removes the use of inventory from the liquidity measurement. It is therefore a more safe or conservative measure. (Section 2.2)

12) Generally speaking, the higher the _____ ratio, the more solvent a company is.

    A) Equity
    B) Debt
    C) Debt to Equity
    D) Fixed Asset

The correct answer is A:) Equity. The equity ratio indicates what portion of assets are financed by equity, which is generally lower cost and does not required fixed charges be paid on a regular basis, which would indicated better solvency. (Section 2.3)

13) The solvency ratio (the actual ratio, not just the class of ratios) is more conservative a measure because it uses _____.

A) Pre-tax earnings plus depreciation
B) EBIT plus depreciation
C) EBT plus depreciation
D) After-tax earnings plus depreciation

The correct answer is D:) After-tax earnings plus depreciation. The solvency ratio uses cash flows to determine how much of a company's earnings are available to cover all debt obligations. It is considered one of the most conservative ways to measure solvency. (Section 2.3)

14) Most investors want to see a _____ ratio that is consistent over time, not changing, as opposed to a high or low ratio.

A) Earnings per share
B) PE Ratio
C) Fixed charges
D) Dividend payout

The correct answer is D:) Dividend payout. The dividend payout ratio is one investors would rather see as stable over time, because it indicates a reliable dividend payment policy. (Section 2.4)

15) Market prospect ratios are the most widely used but also the most _____.

A) Informational when considered alone
B) Consistent over time
C) Reliable when reported by the company
D) Susceptible to influence by accounting conventions

The correct answer is D:) Susceptible to accounting conventions. The way a company recognizes income and whether they have recently repurchased stock can have a major impact on the profitability ratios. These ratios must always be considered comparatively, never alone. (Section 2.4)

16) Profitability ratios are derived from the _____ and _____ statements.

    A) Income; Owner's equity
    B) Income; Balance sheet
    C) Balance sheet; Cash flow
    D) Cash flow; Income

The correct answer is B:) Income; Balance sheet. The profitability ratios are derived from items on the income statement and balance sheet: profits, assets, debts, and equity. (Section 2.5)

17) The DuPont system of analysis indicates that higher ROA can be achieved by _____.

    A) Higher profit margins
    B) Higher debt levels
    C) Higher return on assets
    D) Both A and C

The correct answer is D:) Both A and C. Higher debt levels do not necessarily affect asset levels, and therefore will not have a direct effect on ROA. However, higher debt levels do affect the DuPont ROE. (Section 2.5)

18) The DuPont ROE formula is _____.

    A) ROE x 1 – Debt/Assets
    B) ROA x 1 – Debt/Assets
    C) ROA / 1 – Debt/Assets
    D) ROA x PM x TAT

The correct answer is C:) ROA / 1 – Debt/Assets. By definition, ROE = ROA / 1 –Debt/Assets. (Section 2.5)

19) Two companies, Firm A and Firm B, have the same revenues of $300,000, COGS of $100,000, SG&A of $75,000, but only Firm B has $50,000 in depreciation expense. If both are taxed at 35% corporate tax rate, what is the <u>difference</u> in taxes that they have to pay?

    A) $10,000
    B) $17,500
    C) $26,250
    D) $43,750

The correct answer is B:) $17,500. See the following answer. (Section 3.3)

	Firm A	Firm B
Sales	$300,000	$300,000
COGS	$100,000	$100,000
Op. Profit	$200,000	$200,000
SG&A	$75,000	$75,000
Depreciation	$0	$50,000
EBIT	$125,000	$75,000
Taxes (35%)	$43,750	$26,250

20) Marginal tax rates are _____.

    A) Determined by dividing taxes paid by total taxable income
    B) Not applicable to individuals
    C) The amount of taxes assessed on the next dollar of income
    D) The amount of taxes assessed up to $50,000 of income

The correct answer is C:) The amount of taxes assessed on the next dollar of income. Average taxes are determined by dividing taxes paid by taxable income, marginal tax rates apply to individuals and businesses as of the writing of this text, and marginal tax rates have many brackets, not just up to $50,000. (Section 2.5)

21) Keeping your money under a mattress is _____.

    A) Just as safe as putting it into a savings account
    B) Risky because its value will go down over time
    C) Wise because it's important to save your money
    D) Risky because someone else could easily find it

The correct answer is B:) Risky because its value will go down over time. Keeping money under a mattress is risky because money cannot grow under a mattress. In fact, it is most likely that the value of a dollar is going to shrink over time. (Section 4.1)

22) _____ cost is the loss of money you could have made if you had invested in something productive.

    A) Nominal
    B) Inflation
    C) Time value
    D) Opportunity

The correct answer is D:) Opportunity. When you choose not to put your money to productive use, you lose the money plus whatever money you could have gained otherwise if you chose a different use for the money. (Section 4.1)

23) If you have $2,000 to save for five years at a simple interest rate of 5%, how much in total interest will you earn?

    A) $100
    B) $500
    C) $2,000
    D) $2,500

The correct answer is B:) $500. The question asks for total interest, not total earnings, which would be D. (Section 4.1)

24) When using a financial calculator, if you see a negative sign in front of your answer, what does it mean?

    A) The amount is an outflow of funds.
    B) The amount is an inflow of funds.
    C) The amount is a negative return.
    D) The amount is a positive return.

The correct answer is A:) The amount is an outflow of funds. A negative sign when performing time value of money problems does not mean you have lost that amount of money (a negative return), it means it is the opposite flow of funds from where you started. An inflow would be a positive amount. (Section 4.1)

25) If you have $10,000 to save for six years at a compound interest rate of 4%, what total amount will you have in the future?

    A) $2,624.77
    B) $2,653.19
    C) $12,653.19
    D) $12,624.77

The correct answer is C:) $12,653.19. B shows only the interest earned, A and D used the wrong variables. (Section 4.1)

26) Sir Richard Branson has begun selling tickets to the moon in the year 2025 for a very low price of $150,000. If today is 2019 and you have $50,000 and you can invest this money at an interest rate of 7%, how much more money will you need to earn $150,000 in the future?

   A) $43,412.46
   B) $50,000
   C) $93,412.46
   D) $100,000

The correct answer is A:) $43,412.46. See below for work. Make sure you know exactly what the question is asking. Here you need to find the present value lump sum, then subtract the amount you currently have to determine how much more you would need today. (Section 4.2)

$150,000 = FV
7 = N
7 = I/Y
CPT PV = ? = $93,412.46

$93,412.46 - $50,000 = $43,412.46

27) You have always wanted to buy an SUV, and with a new job you think you will be able to afford $6,000 payments per year. You have found a dealership that will loan you money at a 5% rate of interest over six years. How much of an SUV can you afford today?

   A) $25,274.18
   B) $30,454.15
   C) $36,000.00
   D) $37,800.00

The correct answer is B:) $30,454.15. See below for work. (Section 4.2)

$6,000 = PMT
6 = N
5 = I/Y
PV = ? = $30,454.15

We can see that we could afford an SUV that costs approximately $30,400 with a loan with a 6% annual interest rate.

28) Which of the following is NOT considered an annuity?

    A) A legal settlement of $10,000 per year for five years.
    B) A common stock dividend that grows by 5% and is paid every six months.
    C) A preferred stock dividend that is the same and is paid every quarter.
    D) A retirement account that promises a $4,000 annual payout for twenty years.

The correct answer is B:) A common stock dividend that grows by 5% and is paid every six months. An annuity needs to be an *equal* payment that happens at regular intervals. If a common stock dividend is growing, it will change in amount every six months. (Section 4.2)

29) You need to save $200,000 for your child's college education. They are ten years old and will attend college when they are eighteen. If you can save at an interest rate of 5% annually, how much money do you need today?

    A) $20,994.36
    B) $116,895.87
    C) $83,104.13
    D) $135,367.87

The correct answer is D:) $135,367.87. See below for work. (Section 4.2)

$200,000 = FV
8 = N
5 = I/Y
PV = ? = $135,367.87

30) Your aunt promises to give you $2,000 for the next four years as long as you promise to keep up straight A's in school. You think you can then save that money in an interest bearing savings account at an interest rate of 2.5%. What is the value of your aunt's gift today?

    A) $7,523.95
    B) $15,047.90
    C) $1,811.90
    D) $4,593.19

The correct answer is A:) $7,523.95. See below for work. (Section 4.2)

$2,000 = PMT
4 = N
2.5 = I/Y
PV = ? = $7,523.95

31) You have always wanted to get a dog, but you know the cost of food, vet bills, and boarding when you go away is going to cost at least $1,000 per year. You have saved up $8,000, and the breed you are looking at buying tends to live a very long time, so you want to make sure you are covered for at least the next ten years and are going to save at an interest rate of 3%. How much in annual payments will you earn?

    A) $62.15
    B) $937.84
    C) $1,000.00
    D) $3,216.92

The correct answer is B:) $937.84. See below for work. (Section 4.2)

$8,000 = PV
10 = N
3 = I/Y
PMT = ? = $937.84

32) You work for a company that is trying to determine if they will have enough money in five years to purchase a new computer. The computer will cost $3,000 and they have $2,000 in the bank. They are earning a meager 2.5% on their savings. How much will they have in five years?

    A) $2,250.00
    B) $2,262.82
    C) $3,000.00
    D) $3,216.92

The correct answer is B:) $2,262.82. This will not be enough money. See below for work. (Section 4.3)

$2,000 = PV
5 = N
2.5 = I/Y
FV = ? = $2,262.82

33) You have always wanted to have a very fancy watch. The one you have your eye on is $8,000. You decide you will take on a second job in order to save up for this watch and hope to buy it in five years. You believe you can earn $1,000 per year at 5% interest. Will you have enough money? If not, how much more per month would you need to earn?

    A) Yes. $1,000 per month will be more than enough money.
    B) No. You will need $1,256.87 per month.
    C) No. You will need $1,447.80 per month.
    D) Yes. $1,000 per month is the exact amount you need.

The correct answer is C:) No. You will need $1,447.80 per month. See below for work. (Section 4.3)

In order to solve this problem, you really need one step. Find the payment associated with earning $8,000 in five years at 5%. If that number is greater than $1,000, then you know you need to earn more per month.

$8,000 = FV
5 = N
5 = I/Y
PMT = $1,447.80

34) An annuity whose payments occur at the _____ of the year is known as an ordinary annuity.

    A) Beginning
    B) Ending
    C) Middle
    D) Beginning and ending

The correct answer is A:) Beginning. Ordinary annuities have payments that occur at the end of each time period, usually a year. (Section 4.4)

35) You have $5000 you plan to invest in a savings account. You are considering two banks, one who advertises an ordinary annuity and the other advertises an annuity due. You know you can earn more money in an annuity due, but want to know how much more. If you can earn and interest rate of 6.2% over five years, how much more will you earn with an annuity due?

    A) $1,000.00
    B) $1,754.39
    C) $5,000.00
    D) $6,754.49

The correct answer is B:) $1,754.39. See work below. (Section 4.5)

	Annuity Due	Ordinary Annuity
PMT =	$5,000	$5,000
N =	5	5
I/Y =	6.2	6.2
	BEGIN Mode	END Mode
FV =	$30,052.72	$28,298.23

The difference is how much you will earn: $30,052.72 - $28,298.23 = $1,754.39

36) You have been looking for a new office space to rent and the landlord with whom you just spoke will offer you a discount if you agree to pay the full year upfront. Usually the rent is $500 a month, but she will give you a 10% discount if you pay in full. If interest rates are 5.5%, and you plan to rent for the next four years, what is the value of your rent in the future to the landlord?

    A) $2,552.55
    B) $2,290.55
    C) $24,737.89
    D) $27,567.54

The correct answer is C:) $24,737.89. See work below. (Section 4.5)

BGN Mode
PMT = $500 x 12 = $6,000; $6,000 x .90 = $5,400
N = 4
I/Y = 5.5
FV = $24,737.89

37) All variables being equal, a/an _____ will be worth more in the future.

    A) Ordinary annuity
    B) Annuity due
    C) Both will be equal
    D) There is not enough information to answer

The correct answer is B:) Annuity due. Because we know the annuity due assumes payments occur at the beginning of a time period, if two investments have all the same variables with the exception of timing, the annuity due will always be worth more. (Section 4.5)

38) Your bank is advertising a 5% loan program, only you read the fine print and realize the loan is compounded quarterly. How much will you really be paying in interest per year on an annualized basis?

    A) 5%
    B) 5.02%
    C) 5.09%
    D) 5.25%

The correct answer is C:) 5.09%. See work below. (Section 5.2)

$$EAR = [\ (1 + .05/4)^4]\ -1$$
$$EAR = [1.0125^4]-1$$
$$EAR = [1.0509]-1$$
$$EAR = .0509 \text{ or } 5.09\%$$

39) You just saw a car commercial that announces an introductory APR of 0% for the first three months, with .75% APR per month thereafter. You think this is a great deal, so you quickly calculate the APR on an annual basis and get:

    A) 0.75%
    B) 5.00%
    C) 9.00%
    D) 12.00%

The correct answer is C:) 9.00%. 12 x 0.75% = 9.00%. (Section 5.3)

40) You have decided to purchase a home and the bank is quoting you a 4.5% nominal interest rate on a $200,000 loan. You will also need to pay origination fees of $1,500, mortgage insurance of $2,000, and closing costs of $1,000. What is your APR?

    A) 4.5%
    B) 4.6%
    C) 4.7%
    D) 4.8%

The correct answer is B:) 4.6%. See work below. (Section 5.3)

Total fees: $1,500 + $2,000 + $1,000 = $4,500

$204,500 x 4.5% = $9202.50
$9202.50 / $200,000 = 4.6%

41) Working capital management is the financial management of the _____ of the firm.

    A) Current assets
    B) Current liabilities
    C) Both A and B
    D) Neither

The correct answer is C:) Both A and B. Current assets and liabilities are the primary source of every day "fuel" for the company. (Section 6.1)

42) The best source of internally generated funds for short-term financing needs is _____.

    A) Stockholder's equity
    B) Current liabilities
    C) Fixed assets
    D) Inventory

The correct answer is D:) Inventory. Ideally a company will have enough cash on hand from sales to fund future inventory needs. However, rapid growth almost always means external short-term financing will be needed. (Section 6.2)

43) Using accounts receivable as collateral to secure a loan is known as _____.

    A) Field warehousing
    B) Floor planning
    C) Factoring
    D) Fixed planning

The correct answer is C:) Factoring. This is a form of using accounts receivable as collateral to secure a loan. (Section 6.2)

44) Level production methods are more likely to lead to _____.

    A) Excess cash
    B) Unused capacity
    C) Excess inventory
    D) Lack of fixed assets

The correct answer is C:) Excess inventory. With level production, inventory is made at a consistent pace, which may be independent of demand, and inventory could build up if demand suddenly wanes. (Section 6.4)

45) Just-in-time inventory management _____.

    A) Matches sales and production as closely as possible
    B) Ensures the highest level of internally generated funds
    C) Reduces the need for external financing if done properly
    D) All of the above

The correct answer is D:) All of the above. Just-in-time inventory management, which is the attempt to match sales and production very closely, when done correctly, can increase internally generated funds, thereby reducing reliance on loans or lines of credit. (Section 6.4)

46) If a company has seasonal peaks, their accounts receivable pattern is likely to:

    A) Build up during peak sales and then be reduced as collections occur
    B) Fully fund additional inventory needs
    C) Have a stable level of receivables at all times
    D) None of the above are likely patterns

The correct answer is A:) Build up during peak sales and then be reduced as collections occur. As discussed with a seasonal sales company, as demand and sales peak, so will receivables, which means internally generated funds will not be sufficient to fund additional inventory if needed. (Section 6.5)

47) If a company is extended trade terms of 2/10 net 30, what will they save if they were extended $5,000 on credit and pay on the seventh day?

   A) $50
   B) $100
   C) $150
   D) $200

The correct answer is B:) $100. See work below (Section 6.6)

$5,000 x .98 = $4,900; $5,000 - $4,900 = $100

48) With regard to working capital, a good short-term investment is:

   A) A basic savings account
   B) Extending trade credit
   C) Treasury bills
   D) A bond that matures in five years

The correct answer is C:) Treasury bills. While a basic savings account can be turned into cash in less than a year, it is not considered an investment. Extending trade credit is also not a form of investment, and is more likely to cost money than generate additional income. Treasury bills are highly liquid, provide a guaranteed rate of return, and mature in less than one year (usually 270 days.) A bond that has only one year remaining to maturity could be considered a short-term investment, but a five-year bond is a long-term investment. (Section 6.7)

49) What is the primary purpose of a cash budget?

   A) To keep an account of cash on hand
   B) To assist in determining production needs
   C) To help forecast the borrowing needs, if any, of the firm
   D) All of the above

The correct answer is D:) All of the above. A cash budget is a tool that is used at every step of the working capital management process. Therefore, all aspects of working capital are integrated into the cash budget. (Section 6.8)

50) Complete the cash budget below and determine the amount of borrowing a business needs to maintain a cash balance of $8,000 each month.

	Month 1	Month 2
Net cash flow	$1,000	($3,000)
Beginning cash balance	$8,000	$9,000
Cumulative cash balance	$9,000	$6,000
Loan (Repayment)	$0	?
Cumulative loan balance	$0	?
Ending cash balance	$9,000	$8,000

    A) $0
    B) $1,000
    C) $2,000
    D) $3,000

The correct answer is C:) $2,000. Explanation: The business ends month one with $9,000 in cash. The next month they experience a negative $3,000 in cash flows, leaving them with $6,000 in cash. In order to maintain the $8,000 balance: $8,000 - $6,000 = $2,000. They need to borrow $2,000. (Section 6.8)

51) What is the risk-free rate of return?

    A) It is a guaranteed rate of return for any investment
    B) It is a theoretical rate of return, there are no guarantees
    C) It is the return you can expect for investing in the stock market in general
    D) It is the return you will earn on stable corporate bonds

The correct answer is B:) It is a theoretical rate of return, there are no guarantees. While the risk-free rate of return is often tied to government securities of stable economies, which enjoy a historically stable rate of return, we must be careful to realize there is no absolute guarantee when it comes to investing. (Section 7.1)

52) The increase in the price of a stock is called?

    A) Stock dividend
    B) Capital investment
    C) Capital appreciation
    D) Debenture

The correct answer is C:) Capital appreciation. When something appreciates in value, it is another way of saying it has *increased* in value. Capital is another way of referring to money. (Section 7.1)

53) If a $1,000 face value bond pays a 10% coupon semi-annually, what is the amount of one coupon payment to an investor?

    A) $10
    B) $50
    C) $100
    D) $110

The correct answer is B:) $50. Solution: $1,000 x .10 = $100. $100 paid semi-annually is two payments of $50, so a single payment would be $50. (Section 7.2)

54) What is the present value of a $1,000 face value bond, with a 5% coupon paid annually, ten years to maturity and a yield to maturity of 7%?

    A) $859.53
    B) $1,086.60
    C) $1,154.43
    D) $1,197.10

The correct answer is A:) $859.53. See work below. (Section 7.2)

FV = $1,000
PMT = $50
N = 10
I/Y = 7
PV = ? = -$859.53

55) Which of the following is most likely to issue a debenture?

    A) A new startup company
    B) A company heading into bankruptcy
    C) An unstable government whose country has been at war for several years
    D) A large corporation that has a history of paying on time

The correct answer is D:) A large corporation that has a history of paying on time. Because a debenture is a bond issued with no form of collateral, it is important that the issuer be creditworthy. (Section 7.3)

56) What is the purpose of a sinking fund?

    A) To ensure the bond issue deposits funds to pay down debt immediately
    B) To ensure there is a consistent method of retiring bonds
    C) To ensure a higher interest rate is paid to bondholders
    D) To ensure every bond is held until maturity

The correct answer is B:) To ensure there is a consistent method of retiring bonds. The sinking fund is created specifically to retire bonds before they all reach maturity, and to offer a lower interest rate, not a higher one. Sinking funds do not need to be funded immediately. (Section 7.3)

57) What is the yield on a 6% coupon with a bond trading at $1,112?

    A) 6%
    B) 6.12%
    C) 5%
    D) 5.4%

The correct answer is D:) 5.4%. Solution: $60 / $1,112 = 5.4%. (Section 7.5)

58) What is the price of a stock that has a required rate of return of 8%, will pay a dividend of $4 next year, and has a growth rate of 2%?

    A) $50.00
    B) $51.00
    C) $66.67
    D) $68.00

The correct answer is C:) $66.67 Solution: $4/ .08-.02 = $4/.06 = $66.67. Be careful with the wording in this problem. Notice the dividend figure stated "next year," so you should know that this is D1 and you do not need to determine a new dividend figure here. (Section 7.6)

59) If a stock has variable growth for two years, paying dividends of $5 in year one and $5.50 in year two, and then has 4% growth every year after, what is the present value if the required rate of return is 12%?

    A) $57.00
    B) $64.57
    C) $71.50
    D) $75.00

The correct answer is B:) $64.57. See work below. (Section 7.6)

First we need to find the present value of the dividends:

Year 1: FV = $5.00, N = 1, I/Y = 12, PV = ? = $4.46
Year 2: FV = $5.50, N = 2, I/Y = 12, PV = ? = $4.38

Then we need to find D_3 by multiplying D_2 by the growth rate.

$5.50 x 1.04 = $5.72 = D_3

Then we divide this by (r-g) to get P_2: $5.72 / .12 - .04 = $5.72/.08 = $71.50

Now we find P_2 discounted to P_0:
Price in year 2: FV = $71.50, N = 2, I/Y = 12, PV = ? = $57.00

Now that we have all the values for cash flows in year zero, we total them to get P_0:

$57.00 + $4.46 + 4.38 = $64.57

60) The process of planning for expenditures greater than one year is known as:

    A) Working capital management
    B) Fixed asset management
    C) Current asset management
    D) Capital budgeting

The correct answer is D:) Capital budgeting. Capital budgeting is the process of planning for expenditures and investments that will last longer than one year. While fixed assets are involved, they are not the only aspect of capital budgeting to consider. There are investments in securities, as well as the financing needs, by issuing stocks and bonds. (Section 8.1)

61) When a company must decide between two projects and cannot spend capital on both, it is known as a _____ decision.

A) Inclusive
B) Mutually exclusive
C) Independent
D) Fixed

The correct answer is B:) Mutually exclusive. This is when a company must choose between competing projects and define the strategic vision of the business. (Section 8.2)

62) If a company has EBITDA of $20,000, tax rate of 40%, and depreciation expense of $20,000, what is their cash flow?

A) -$20,000
B) -$0
C) $10,000
D) $20,000

The correct answer is D:) $20,000. See work below. As can be seen, if EBITDA and depreciation allowance are equal, there is no income to tax, and cash flow is positive $20,000 because it was never spent. (Section 8.4)

EBITDA	$20,000
Depreciation	$20,000
EBIT	$0
Taxes (30%)	$0
EAT	$0
Depreciation	$20,000
Cash Flow	**$20,000**

63) If a company currently earns cash flows of $25,000, and is considering a project that will increase their cash flows to $55,000, what is their incremental cash flow?

A) $25,000
B) $30,000
C) $35,000
D) $40,000

The correct answer is B:) $30,000. New project – current operations = incremental cash flow. $55,000 - $25,000 = $30,000 (Section 8.5)

64) ABC Corporation's current revenues are $100,000 and expenses are $35,000 per year. They are considering taking on a new project and buying new equipment for $5,000, which will increase annual revenues by $20,000 by increasing production, but also increase expenses by $10,000. What is their net incremental cash flow in the first year (before taxes and depreciation)?

    A) $5,000
    B) $10,000
    C) $20,000
    D) $15,000

The correct answer is A:) $5,000. See work below. (Section 8.5)

Change in revenues: $20,000
Change in expenses: $10,000
Initial outlay: $5,000

Incremental cash flow: $20,000 - $10,000 - $5,000 = $5,000

65) Currently XYZ, Inc. has revenues of $50,000 and expenses of $10,000. They plan to purchase equipment for $25,000, which will increase their revenues to $100,000 and their expenses to $25,000. What is their incremental cash flow in the first year (before taxes and depreciation)?

    A) $5,000
    B) $10,000
    C) $50,000
    D) $75,000

The correct answer is B:) $10,000. See work below. (Section 8.5)

Change in revenue: $100,000 - $50,000 = $50,000 (increase)
Change in expenses: $25,000 - $10,000 = $15,000 (increase)
Initial outlay: $25,000

Incremental cash flow: $50,000 - $15,000 - $25,000 = $10,000

66) Discounting the future cash flows of a project to the present time and comparing them to the initial outlay needed to fund the project is known as _____.

    A) Time value of money
    B) Increment cash flow
    C) Net present value
    D) Depreciation

The correct answer is C:) Net present value. Time value of money is a tool we use in the discounting process to determine net present value. Incremental cash flows are the figures we actually discount. (Section 8.6)

67) Depreciating the value of an asset equally over a set number of years is known as _____.

    A) MACRS depreciation
    B) Incremental depreciation
    C) Straight line depreciation
    D) Non-cash depreciation

The correct answer is C:) Straight line depreciation. MACRS depreciation allows a greater deduction in the early years of owning the asset. (Section 8.6)

68) If a company purchases equipment costing $150,000 and depreciates it straight line over five years, has a tax rate of 20% and EBITDA of $52,000 each year, what is the annual cash flow? (Hint: you need to construct a pro forma cash flow.)

    A) $17,600
    B) $30,000
    C) $47,600
    D) $50,000

The correct answer is C:) $47,600. See work below. (Section 8.7)

	Year 1	Year 2	Year 3	Year 4	Year 5
EBITDA	$52,000	$52,000	$52,000	$52,000	$52,000
Depreciation	$30,000	$30,000	$30,000	$30,000	$30,000
EBT	$22,000	$22,000	$22,000	$22,000	$22,000
Taxes (20%)	$4,400	$4,400	$4,400	$4,400	$4,400
EAT	$17,600	$17,600	$17,600	$17,600	$17,600
+ Depreciation	$30,000	$30,000	$30,000	$30,000	$30,000
Cash Flow	**$47,600**	**$47,600**	**$47,600**	**$47,600**	**$47,600**

69) If a company purchases equipment costing $150,000 and has cash flows of $25,000 for the next five years, at a discount rate of 5%, should they undertake the project? (Round to the nearest dollar.)

    A) Yes, the project is profitable, earning $108,238
    B) No, the project is not profitable, earning -$41,762
    C) Yes, the project is profitable, earning $41,762
    D) There is not enough information to tell

The correct answer is B:) No, the project is not profitable, earning -$41,762. See work below. (Section 8.9)

Cash Flow Year 1: FV = $25,000, N = 1, I/Y = 5, PV = $23,810
Cash Flow Year 2: FV = $25,000, N = 2, I/Y = 5, PV = $22,676
Cash Flow Year 3: FV = $25,000, N = 3, I/Y = 5, PV = $21,596
Cash Flow Year 4: FV = $25,000, N = 4, I/Y = 5, PV = $20,568
Cash Flow Year 5: FV = $25,000, N = 5, I/Y = 5, PV = $19,588

Total present value of cash flows: $108,238

$108,238 - $150,000 = -$41,762

70) The capital budgeting method that prioritizes recouping costs as soon as possible is:

    A) Net present value
    B) Internal rate of return
    C) Accounting rate of return
    D) Payback

The correct answer is D:) Payback. This is the simplest way to determine if a project will be accepted—how soon you get your money back. (Section 8.10)

71) A company has earnings after taxes of $15,000 in year one, $16,500 in year two, and $22,000 in year three. If their initial outlay was $75,000, what is their accounting rate of return?

    A) 17.83%
    B) 23.78%
    C) 42.78%
    D) 71.33%

The correct answer is B:) 23.78%. See work below. (Section 8.11)

Total EAT: $15,000 + $16,500 + $22,000 = $53,500
Average EAT: $53,500 / 3 = $17,833.33

Accounting rate of return = $17,833.33 / $75,000 = 23.78%

72) What is the IRR if a company has the following cash flows?

	Cash flows
Year 0	($100,000)
Year 1	$25,000
Year 2	$32,000
Year 3	$22,000
Year 4	$18,000
Year 5	$15,000
Year 6	$10,000

    A) 7.14%
    B) 8.00%
    C) 17.14%%
    D) 22.00%

The correct answer is A:) 7.14%. See work below. (Section 8.12)

Then enter CF $100,000 S ENTER #
$25,000 ENTER ##
$32,000 ENTER ##
$22,000 ENTER ##
$18,000 ENTER ##
$15,000 ENTER ##
$10,000 ENTER ##

Then press IRR and CPT and you get 7.14%.

73) The point where revenues equal expenses is called:

A) Profit point
B) Net present value
C) Fixed income point
D) Break-even point

The correct answer is D:) Break-even point. This is where there are zero profits and, by definition, revenues are equal to (or even with) expenses. (Section 8.13)

74) Alpha Beta Co. makes wooden alphabet puzzles. They just bought a new machine to produce the puzzles faster, which cost them $15,000. They sell their puzzles for $24 per unit and their costs are $12 per unit. What is their break-even point?

A) 250 units
B) 600 units
C) 1,250 units
D) 1,850 units

The correct answer is C:) 1,250 units. $15,000 / ($24-$12) = $15,000/$12 = $1,250. (Section 8.13)

75) Do Si Do, Co. makes dance shoes. They just bought a new machine to improve the manner and speed with which they stitch the fabric to their soles, which cost them $25,000. They sell their shoes for $34.50 per pair and their costs are now decreased to $8 per unit. What is their break-even point? (Round to the next highest unit.)

A) 725 units
B) 944 units
C) 1,250 units
D) 3,125 units

The correct answer is B:) 944 units. $25,000 / ($34.50-$8) = $25,000/$26.50 = 943. (Section 8.13)

76) The required rate of return on common stock or the yield to maturity on a bond are _____ to the company.

    A) Costs
    B) Profits
    C) Investments
    D) Risks

The correct answer is A:) Costs. The returns stockholders and bondholders expect are costs to the company. (Section 9.1)

77) Suppose the Twin Stars Co. has bonds outstanding with a face value of $1,000, eight years to maturity, a coupon rate of 6%, a present value of $1,100, and a tax rate of 25%. What is the cost of debt to the company? (Hint: don't forget the tax effects of interest payments.)

    A) 3.36%
    B) 4.48%
    C) 4.72%
    D) 3.54%

The correct answer is A:) 3.36%. See work below. (Section 9.2)

$1,000 = FV
8 = N
$60 = PMT
-$1,100 = PV
YTM = ? = 4.48%

4.48% x (1-.25) = 4.48% x .75 = 3.36%

78) If Turtle Dove Inc. has bonds outstanding selling for $840, with a yield to maturity of 8.7%, a coupon rate of 5%, and a corporate tax rate of 20%, what is their cost of debt?

   A) 5.00%
   B) 6.96%
   C) 8.70%
   D) 9.54%

The correct answer is B:) 6.96%. Due to the fact that the yield to maturity is given to us, we can ignore some of the extra information given to us. The calculation is simply the YTM x (1- Tax rate) 8.7% x (1-.20) = 8.7% x .80 = 6.98. (Section 9.2)

79) The _____ a company is, the higher their cost of debt will likely be.

   A) More profitable
   B) More leveraged
   C) Higher taxed
   D) Less leveraged

The correct answer is B:) More leveraged. Profits will not directly affect cost of debt. Leveraged firms hold more debt in general, which raises the cost of debt because of the likelihood of paying all debt obligation on time, in full, decreasing the more debt a company has. Higher taxes would actually decrease the cost of debt through increasing the tax deduction amount. (Section 9.2)

80) If a stock just paid a dividend of $3.25, is priced at $42, and expects a growth rate of 4.5% in the future, what is the cost of equity?

   A) 4.5%
   B) 7.74%
   C) 12.24%
   D) 12.60%

The correct answer is D:) 12.60%. See work below. (Section 9.4)

$D0 = \$3.25$; $D1 = \$3.25 \times 1.045 = \$3.40$
$r = (\$3.40 / \$42) + .045 = 12.60\%$

81) Determine the cost of equity on a stock that expects to pay a dividend of $4.32 next year, has a growth rate of 5.17%, and a current price of $37.50.

    A) 7.74%
    B) 11.52%
    C) 12.60%
    D) 16.69%

The correct answer is D:) 16.69%. See work below. (Section 9.4)

$r = (\$4.32 / \$37.50) + .0517 = 16.69\%$

82) A preferred stock pays a dividend of $4 and is priced at $56, what is the cost of preferred equity?

    A) 4.5%
    B) 7.14%
    C) 12.24%
    D) 12.60%

The correct answer is B:) 7.14%. $4/$56 = 7.14%. (Section 9.4)

83) A preferred stock is trading at $84 and pays a dividend of $5, what is the cost of preferred stock to the company?

    A) 6.00%
    B) 7.14%
    C) 12.24%
    D) 12.00%

The correct answer is A:) 6.00%. $5/$84 = 6.00%. (Section 9.4)

84) The total cost a company must pay to fund any project is known as the _____.

    A) Hurdle rate
    B) Discount rate
    C) Weighted average cost of capital
    D) All of the above

The correct answer is D:) All of the above. Each of these terms can be used to describe the cost of capital of a company to fund their projects. (Section 9.5)

85) Suppose a company has debt in the amount of $150 million, equity of $105 million, and preferred stock of $65 million. The bonds outstanding have a face value of $1,000, have twelve years left to maturity, a coupon of 8.5%, and are being sold in the market for $980. The common stock is selling at a price of $85, with the most recent dividend paid of $3.64, and a projected growth rate of 4.5% in the future. The preferred stock price is $50 and the dividend is $3.25, indefinitely. With a tax rate of 20%, what is this company's weight average cost of capital?

    A) 5.04%
    B) 7.62%
    C) 8.4%
    D) 9.0%

The correct answer is B:) 7.62%. See work below. (Section 9.5)

First determine the weights:

Total capital: $150 + $105 + $65 = $320

Weight of debt = $150/$320 = 46.88%
Weight of equity = $105/$320 = 32.81%
Weight of preferred stock = $65/$320 = 20.31%

Now find the cost of each source of capital:

$1,000 = FV
12 = N
$85 = PMT
-$980 = PV
I/Y = 8.8%

After-tax cost of debt = 8.8% x (1-.20) = 8.8% x .80 = 7.04%

Cost of equity:

r = (($3.64 x 1.045) /$85) + .045 = ($3.80/$85) + .045 = .045 + .045 = 9.0%

Cost of preferred stock:

r = $3.25/$50 = 6.5%

WACC = (.4688 x .0704) + (.3281 x .09) + (.2031 x .065)
      = (.033) + (.03) + (.0132)
      = 7.62%

86) The idea that the greater the risk, the greater the reward or loss, and the less risk, the less reward or loss is known as _____.

    A) Risky business
    B) Risk and reward tradeoff
    C) Cost of capital
    D) Time value of money

The correct answer is B:) Risk and reward tradeoff. While business can involve many types of risk, the official term for the relationship between risk and reward is risk and reward tradeoff. (Section 10.1)

87) Find the standard deviation of the following data set:

Data Points
3
4
6
2
3

    A) 3.00
    B) 3.16
    C) 10.00
    D) 10.16

The correct answer is B:) 3.16. See work below. (Section 10.3)

Data Points	Mean	Variance	Variance Squared
3	4	-1	1
4	4	0	0
6	4	2	4
2	4	-2	4
3	4	-1	1
		Total	10

Square root of 10 = 3.1623

88) If the risk free rate is 3%, inflation is 2%, the default-risk premium for a bond is 5%, and the maturity risk premium is 2%, what is the total expected rate of return bondholders are expecting from this bond?

A) 5%
B) 7%
C) 10%
D) 12%

The correct answer is D:) 12%. We simply add all components together: 3% + 2% + 5% + 2% = 12%. (Section 10.4)

89) If the nominal rate is 10% and inflation is 2%, what is the real interest rate?

A) 2%
B) 5%
C) 8%
D) 10%

The correct answer is C:) 8%. We subtract the inflation rate from the nominal rate to determine the real interest rate. 10% - 2% = 8% (Section 10.5)

90) If a stock's beta is .98, the risk free rate is 3%, and the expected return on the market is 10%, what is the stock's expected return?

A) 3.00%
B) 7.00%
C) 9.86%
D) 10.00%

The correct answer is C:) 9.86%. We use the CAPM to solve this problem. Er = .03 + .98(.10-.03) = .03 + .0686 = 9.85% (Section 10.6)

91) When the capital asset pricing model is graphed, what is the line that is created called?

A) Price line
B) Security market line
C) Capital budget line
D) Risk line

The correct answer is B:) Security market line. By definition, the plotted points of the CAPM are called the SML. (Section 10.7)

92) Risk that cannot be diversified by selecting a variety of investments is known as _____ risk.

    A) Specific risk
    B) Systematic risk
    C) Unsystematic risk
    D) Risk premium

The correct answer is B:) Systematic risk. Also known as market risk, systematic risk is the risk inherent in investing in the stock market and cannot be diversified away. (Section 10.8)

93) The concept of spreading your investment among a wider variety of dissimilar investments is called:

    A) Standard deviation
    B) Systematic investing
    C) Risk aversion
    D) Diversification

The correct answer is D:) Diversification. Someone who is risk averse should diversify, but risk aversion is a state, not a strategy. (Section 10.8)

94) It is believed that the 2008 international economic crisis was largely started by the _____ crisis.

    A) Standard deviation
    B) Subprime mortgage
    C) International currency
    D) Exchange rate

The correct answer is B:) Subprime mortgage. The popular practice of bundling subprime mortgages and giving them high credit ratings led to the loss of trillions of dollars as individuals defaulted on their mortgages. (Section 11.1)

95) A _____ exchange rate system is where prices are determined by supply and demand for the currency, and is adopted by most nations.

A) Floating
B) Subprime
C) International
D) Fixed

The correct answer is A:) Floating. Fixed exchange systems are where the government determines currency prices. (Section 11.2)

96) Imagine a U.S. investor has purchased a $1,000 bond from a British company who pays in pounds, and offers a coupon of 6%. At the time of purchase, the exchange rate was $1 = 1 pound. Two years later, the exchange rate is now $1 = .88 pounds. How much is the same coupon payment now worth in dollars?

A) $88.00
B) $52.80
C) $60.00
D) $72.80

The correct answer is B:) $52.80. To solve for U.S. dollars, multiply the coupon payment by the new exchange rate of .88. $60 x .88 = $52.80 (Section 11.3)

97) Imagine a U.S. investor has purchased a $1,000 bond from a Swedish company who pays in francs, and offers a coupon of 7%. At the time of purchase, the exchange rate was $1 = 1 franc. One year later, the exchange rate is now $1 = .95 francs. How much is the same coupon payment now worth in dollars?

A) $88.00
B) $78.95
C) $71.25
D) $72.80

The correct answer is C:) $71.25. To solve for U.S. dollars, multiply the coupon payment by the new exchange rate of .95. $70 x .95 = $71.25 (Section 11.3)

98) Risk that arises due to instability or government policies in a certain country is known as:

A) Currency risk
B) Systematic risk
C) Political risk
D) Company specific risk

The correct answer is C:) Political risk. Currency exchange rates and systematic risk may be affected by political risk, and specific companies may be more or less subject to political risk, but political risk itself is due to the actions of governments, specifically. (Section 11.3)

99) By looking at the following spot and forward rate table, the market expects the pound will _____ relative to the U.S. dollar.

Rates	Pounds/USD
Spot	1.50
30 day forward	1.48
60 day forward	1.47

A) Appreciate
B) Depreciate
C) Stay the same
D) Not enough information

The correct answer is B:) Depreciate. Over the next sixty days, the U.S. dollar will be able to purchase more pounds. (Section 11.5)

100) The ability to buy a contract to lock in the price of a currency at some point in the future is known as:

A) Hedging
B) Betting
C) Leveraging
D) Valuing

The correct answer is A:) Hedging. While some people may think locking in prices in the future can be a form of leverage or betting, the practice is formally known as hedging. (Section 11.6)

Test-Taking Strategies

Here are some test-taking strategies that are specific to this test and to other DSST tests in general:

- Keep your eyes on the time. Pay attention to how much time you have left.

- Read the entire question and read all the answers. Many questions are not as hard to answer as they may seem. Sometimes, a difficult sounding question really only is asking you how to read an accompanying chart. Chart and graph questions are on most DANTES/DSST tests and should be an easy free point.

- If you don't know the answer immediately, the new computer-based testing lets you mark questions and come back to them later if you have time.

- Read the wording carefully. Some words can give you hints to the right answer. There are no exceptions to an answer when there are words in the question such as always, all or none. If one of the answer choices includes most or some of the right answers, but not all, then that is not the answer. Here is an example:

    The primary colors include all of the following:

    A) Red, Yellow, Blue, Green

    B) Red, Green, Yellow

    C) Red, Orange, Yellow

    D) Red, Yellow, Blue

Although item A includes all the right answers, it also includes an incorrect answer, making it incorrect. If you didn't read it carefully, was in a hurry, or didn't know the material well, you might fall for this.

- Make a guess on a question that you do not know the answer to. There is no penalty for an incorrect answer. Eliminate the answer choices that you know are incorrect. For example, this will let your guess be a 1 in 3 chance instead.

Test Preparation

How much you need to study depends on your knowledge of a subject area. If you are interested in literature, took it in school, or enjoy reading then your study and preparation for the literature or humanities test will not need to be as intensive as that of someone who is new to literature.

This book is much different than the regular DANTES study guides. This book actually teaches you the information that you need to know to pass the test. If you are particularly interested in an area, or feel that you want more information, do a quick search online. We've tried not to include too much depth in areas that are not as essential on the test. Everything in this book will be on the test. It is important to understand all major theories and concepts listed in the table of contents. It is also important to know any bolded words.

Don't worry if you do not understand or know a lot about the area. With minimal study, you can complete and pass the test.

Legal Note

FLASHCARDS

This section contains flashcards for you to use to further your understanding of the material and test yourself on important concepts, names or dates. Read the term or question then flip the page over to check the answer on the back. Keep in mind that this information may not be covered in the text of the study guide. Take your time to study the flashcards, you will need to know and understand these concepts to pass the test.

Liquid assets

Fixed assets

The income statement is a measure of

Operating income is determined by

Statement of owner's equity includes net profits or losses and

Solvency is linked to

Profitability ratios are derived from

DuPont ROE formula

Property, plant, and equipment

Current assets

Gross profit minus (SG&A and depreciation expense)

Profitability

Equity

Owner's contributions of capital

ROA / 1 – Debt/Assets

Income and balance sheet

Marginal tax rates	**Opportunity cost**
Beginning annuity payments occur when?	**Just-in-time inventory management**
Net present value	**Depreciating the value of an asset equally over a set number of years**
Total liabilities + Owner's Equity =	**COGS**

The loss of money you could have made if you had invested in something productive

The amount of taxes assessed on the next dollar of income

The attempt to match sales and production

At the beginning of the term

Straight line depreciation

Discounting the future cash flows of a project to the present time and comparing them to the initial outlay needed to fund the project

Cost of goods sold

Total assets

EBIT

EBT

EAT

SG&A

Quick ratio

Times interest earned =

Solvency ratio =

Dividend yield =

Earnings before taxes

Earnings before interest and taxes

Selling, general, and administrative expenses

Earnings after taxes

EBIT / Interest

(Current Assets – Inventory) / Current Liabilities

Cash dividends per share / Price per share

Net income plus depreciation / Total Debt

Made in the USA
Lexington, KY
25 October 2019